new hotel

David Collins
new hotel
architecture and design

conran
OCTOPUS

I would like to dedicate this book to all the underpaid, overworked designers, who slave away for demanding hotel operators and do their best to satisfy the impossible to please. In helping me write this book I owe a great debt to Sam, Jodi, Iain and to everyone at Conran Octopus.

First published in 2001 by
Conran Octopus Limited
a part of Octopus Publishing Group
2–4 Heron Quays, London E14 4JP
www.conran-octopus.co.uk

Reprinted in 2002 (twice)

Publishing Director: Lorraine Dickey
Commissioning Editor: Bridget Hopkinson
Additional text written by: Sam Le Quesne
Copy Editor: Libby Willis

Creative Director: Leslie Harrington
Senior Art Editor: Carl Hodson
Freelance Designer: Isobel de Cordova
Picture Research Manager: Rosanna Peers
Picture Research: Nadine Bazar

Production Director: Zoë Fawcett

British Library Cataloguing-in-Publication Data.
A catalogue record for this book is available from the British Library.

ISBN 1 84091 159 X

Printed in Europe

contents

New Hotel is a snapshot of new design solutions

and trends in contemporary hotel design; it is not a travelogue or a list of my favourite hotel destinations. I have carefully focused on the main elements that shape our perceptions of hotels, what projects their images and what locates them in their various marketplaces. My book concentrates on interior design as opposed to architecture because although some notable architectural statements have been made in purpose-built hotels, I have found that there is often an imbalance between the exterior and interior design in these buildings. Some of the most contemporary buildings I have seen have been lumbered with disappointingly banal and derivative interior design. Conversely, I have found existing buildings that have been sensitively and imaginatively converted to provide exciting new design statements.

The rise of the 'branded hotel' is evident when charting the influence of the Aman hotels or Four Seasons hotels. On the other hand, the 'nonbrand' hotel has become a marketing tool as hotels seek to enhance their status by seeming to be independent. Hotels want to be seen as fashionable, but, in reality, the costs of construction and the length of time required to defray hefty expenditure result in a degree of safety and predictability in the middle road of design, where innovation is restricted by fear of costly mistakes.

In these pages I have tried to be objective about design in order to increase understanding of how the industry can learn from people's mistakes and from their successes. I have broken down the process into manageable sections in order to guide designers and operators through the entire process, and, crucially, to help them arrive at their own conclusions about the merits of the different designers' work.

I would like to thank everyone at Conran Octopus for their invaluable support and enthusiasm during the production of this book.

introduction

a historical perspective

'The divide between the very earliest hotels and the new hotel is vast, but it is understanding the precise nature of this divide that enables us to define the new hotel.'

Left *Built as an inn in 1532, the Lygon Arms, England, is one of the country's oldest hotels. The mellow Cotswold stone, Tudor architecture and imposing carved entrance hark back to the reign of Henry VIII, while antique furniture and period details inside reinforce the air of time-honoured hospitality.*

Opposite *Since its opening in 1906 the Ritz has been – literally – synonymous with opulent luxury. Recently regilded and refurbished, this Rolls-Royce of London hotels continues to offer exclusivity and glamour to its wealthy, sophisticated clientele.*

Newness and modernity are terms that cannot be fully understood nor properly defined without at least a glancing reference to the events of the past. This general truth is particularly relevant to architecture and design, where the themes of former periods become the catalysts for contemporary ideas, as they are continually refreshed and reinvented to suit the social and political zeitgeist.

It would, however, be unrealistic to attempt an exhaustive analysis of all the social and architectural developments that have led to the breed of new hotel that will be discussed in this book. Entire volumes have been devoted to the subject and it cannot simply be dispensed with in the opening chapter. The purpose of this book is to consider the architecture and design of certain contemporary hotels in relation to the aspirations and demands of today's consumers. In order to take on such a large subject,however, some background information is necessary; namely how the hotel has responded to changes in consumer demand over the centuries.

Consumer demand is a deceptively simple term and one that is very much of our time. It denotes a complex

phenomenon that evolved over hundreds of years of a gradual process of social change and reform; it implies an element of choice as well as necessity. The twenty-first-century consumer regards the hotel as a luxury commodity, an opportunity to buy into a lifestyle to which he or she aspires. And it is only by understanding the origins of this demand for quality and style – even status – that the function of the new hotel can be properly put into context.

Early hotels

Consider, for example, the most primitive ancestor of the modern hotel, the inn or boarding-house. Inextricably linked to developments in trade and transportation, the archetypal inn was a simple rest stop, often a room above a pub or in a private residence, and amounting to little more than a place to spend the night before resuming the onward journey. There were, of course, some slightly grander variations, a number of which, such as the Lygon Arms in the English Cotswolds village of Broadway, continue to thrive today.

The Lygon Arms is now owned by the Savoy Group and is trading well on its historical and architectural merit; it is considered by its predominantly upmarket clientele to be a classy rustic retreat. But it is probably reasonable to assume that the wool merchants, migrants and messengers of the sixteenth century who trudged up and down the muddy trade route linking England and Wales saw the Lygon Arms in a rather different light. They definitely were not roused of a morning by the discreet knock of room service ready to place fresh coffee, croissants and a newspaper on the bedside table. In fact, the divide between the functionality of the very earliest hotels and the new hotel is vast, but it is understanding the precise nature of this divide that enables us to define the new hotel and its proper place in the history of the hotel.

Escapism and fantasy

The fact that the inns, boarding-houses and early hotels of the sixteenth and seventeenth centuries were seen as mere necessities is a crucial distinction. They came into being only as by-products of highways, ports, improving travel networks and the resultant need to accommodate an increase in human traffic. Their relation to the new hotel is only a very distant one. True, both served or serve the same fundamental ends of lodging and feeding their guests, but the new hotel has resulted from an entirely different need: the need to escape. Escapism and fantasy were totally absent from the earliest incarnations of the hotel, which were driven by necessity and functionality. It was not until the eighteenth century and the advent of the grand hotel that these factors emerged, and it was at this point that the embryo of the new hotel was formed.

This is a vital development that should be kept in mind throughout the remaining chapters, and one that requires some explanation. For the most part this book will be dedicated to the micro-view of the new hotel, the business of

Opposite *Classical statues, crystal chandeliers and gilded furniture upholstered in precious Como silk testify to the grand heritage of the Villa d'Este beside Lake Como, Italy. One of the most magnificent grand hotels of the nineteenth century, the Villa d'Este provided an atmosphere of pure luxury and escapism for a well-heeled clientele.*
Right *Gleaming lifts lined with walnut veneer glide silently between floors at the Hôtel de Vendôme, Paris, and ever-attentive staff spirit delicacies up and down marble staircases to satisfy guests' every wish.*

briefly, a lifestyle that is glamorous, fashionable and exclusive. It is not just a change of scene but an opportunity to borrow a lifestyle and an image – even a temporary identity – that is more alluring than the reality of a person's life.

The grand hotel

It is therefore necessary to return to the emergence of the grand hotel, the ersatz palace or château rooted in the history of a class and culture that have always been associated with extravagance, indulgence and escapism. The appearance of the grand hotel in Europe from the eighteenth century onwards was not a result of the advances in transportation and the diversification of international trade, as with the earlier inns and boarding-houses; instead it was an inevitable consequence of social and political change.

Revolutions and the tumults of history gradually transformed many of the castles and palaces of Europe into public monuments. They no longer provided the settings for lavish masked balls, receptions and significant political events but were diminished in status to inert museums, remnants of a bygone era. However, the public thirst for glamorous social occasions and the need for splendid venues in which to conduct affairs of state or greet visiting dignitaries were not swept away by the tide of social change. The inspired solution was the grand hotel.

Although the opulence and architectural ostentation of the grand hotel may at first glance seem unrelated – indeed diametrically opposed – to the new hotel (whose often spare, minimalist interiors and sleek modern lines are so much more understated), in fact they are closely linked. The need for escape, indulgence and zeitgeist surroundings is the same, as are the fashionable connotations of such a place. The grand hotel became a haven for the sophisticated, status-conscious traveller and as such bore many hallmarks of the contemporary urban hotel discussed later in this book.

Competition and rivalry

The common goal of alluring the trendsetters of the time meant that the grand hotels were rivals competing for the same niche market. Competition was fierce, just as it is today, and those hotels that survived did so through promotional activities adopted to position them at the cutting edge.

The intense competition at the beginning of the twentieth century between the Hôtel des Bains and the Excelsior in Venice is a particularly dramatic illustration of this. In 1901 the

comparing the minutiae of different designs and architectural approaches that distinguish one establishment from the next. Each has its own identity, and the overall purpose is to illustrate the diversity of views that designers and architects take when considering the contemporary hotel and its target audience. Nevertheless it is still imperative to keep in mind the macro-view. This view sees one common factor, one broad brushstroke characterizing the new hotel as a genre, whether it is London's sleek and minimal Hempel or the majestic SoHo Grand in New York. That factor is escapism.

'Although the opulence and architectural ostentation of the grand hotel may at first seem unrelated to the new hotel, in fact they are closely linked... The grand hotel became a haven for the sophisticated, status-conscious traveller and as such bore many hallmarks of the contemporary urban hotel.'

The term escapism is not used in this context in its most literal or simplistic form – that is, the need to escape and find a change of scene – although that is undeniably a part of the attraction of any hotel. Rather, what separates the new hotel from just any hotel is the extra dimension of escapism that it offers its guests, namely the chance to experience, however inaugural ceremony of the Hôtel des Bains kickstarted a renaissance of the elitism and exclusivity once associated with the royal court. Its location, the Lido, became a mini social court, the epicentre of social snobbery and, above all, the place to be seen. But a few years later, in 1907, the Excelsior dazzled that same fickle crowd who frequented the Hôtel des Bains with an unprecedented display of pyrotechnics, music and festivities that was watched and enjoyed by 30,000 of Venice's bright young things. Then, when Thomas Mann used the Hôtel des Bains as inspiration for *Death in Venice*, the fortunes of this little war took yet another turn. Clearly a new breed of hotel was beginning to flourish, one that was no longer content to be just the barometer of change, reflecting shifts in society and the infrastructures of business and travel. Instead the grand hotel was actually influencing taste, style and social fashions. In short, the prototype of the new urban hotel had arrived.

Travel and the emergence of the urban hotel

Naturally the influence of the expanding Victorian railway networks also has its place in the history of the modern urban hotel. Consider the examples of railway-linked hotels in London alone: the Midlands Hotel at St Pancras Station, the Great Western Hotel at Paddington Station, the Charing Cross Hotel, and the Grosvenor beside Victoria Station. In addition, many hotels were opened to coincide with major events that would attract a great number of visitors. The Great Western Hotel, for example, opened to the public in 1851, the same year that six million visitors descended on the capital to see the Great Exhibition in Hyde Park. This phenomenon was not unique to Britain; similar cases occurred throughout the world. For example, the Hotel Terminus next to the Gare St-Lazare in Paris opened during the Paris International Exhibition in 1889.

A significant result of all this change was that a new species of traveller began to emerge in answer to this new breed

Opposite *Presiding over the Venice Lido, the Hôtel des Bains was the place to be seen at the beginning of the twentieth century. Its Palladian colonnades and cream façade still embody the cultured opulence of the Belle Epoque.*
Right *The Midlands Hotel, at St Pancras Station, London, is a magnificent example of the Victorian railway hotel. In an age of imperialism and expansionism, its scale and ornate furnishings reflected the self-confidence of a prosperous nation.*

of hotel. And this species would soon evolve into the sophisticated modern consumer that wields the spending power in today's market.

The grand tour

This link can be traced as far back as the mid-eighteenth century, when the concept of what became known as the grand tour first began to take a firm hold on the upper classes of British society. At the outset these tourists were almost exclusively young gentlemen who, having finished their classical education, considered it an important rite of passage to tour Europe in order to immerse themselves in the antique culture of its great towns and cities. Many returned bearing classical statues and paintings to adorn their country houses and brought with them a revived interest in the classical styles of such great architects as the Italian Andrea Palladio; neoclassicism became firmly established as the leading

Above *A pioneer in London's financial Square Mile, the Great Eastern Hotel woos its clientele with an aura of exclusivity and professionalism reminiscent of the neighbouring international banks. The sleek reception desk is counterbalanced by a display of contemporary ceramics, however, signalling to potential guests that this is much more than just an ordinary business hotel.* **Right** *The new breed of hotel is defined by its approach to design. The moment guests step inside the lobby of the Delano, Miami, they are confronted by Philippe Starck's modern take on the wood-panelled wall and an elongated orange chaise-longue. The design implies that a very different kind of experience awaits hotel guests and the style elite can feel reassured that they have indeed arrived in the right place.*

fashion of the day. The grand tour soon became a customary fixture in the lives of most well-heeled Europeans.

Even so, at this time travelling conditions were still not much better than basic and things had to evolve quickly to create the kind of facilities that travellers of this class expected. Roads were beginning to improve substantially but the most interesting developments were those that specifically targeted these early tourists.

The popular guidebook

In the late eighteenth century one of the major weapons of the modern traveller was first assembled: the guidebook. This reflects the beginning of an important process. The increasing volume of guidebooks, travel supplements and online information has been one of the key factors in creating the informed, empowered and sophisticated consumer of the twenty-first century and, as such, represents a significant development in terms of the history behind the new hotel.

Guidebooks had existed before, of course, but they were mostly pompous and didactic volumes, awash with sermonizing passages concerning, for example, local customs. But towards the end of the eighteenth century books like *A Gentleman's Guide in his Tour Through Italy* began to appear. The author, Thomas Martyn, was adamant that his guidebook should avoid the pitfalls of other publications of the time. Most travel books were evidently intended to be read by the fireside at home and Martyn clearly considered them to be of little help. He achieved his aim to produce a practical guide, and *Martyn's Gentleman's Guide* resembles the modern travel guidebook very closely in both format and content.

The grand tourist

During the first half of the nineteenth century another decisive characteristic of the modern consumer appeared. Up until this time Europe had been the automatic destination choice for any respectable grand tour, unless circumstances created good reasons for travelling further afield. Gradually, of course, the idea of a grand tour around all the classic European ports of call started to become rather commonplace. In fact many considered it a bit of a cliché. Naturally, then, the fashionable tourists of the day wanted to carve out their own niche, so they started to look beyond the beaten track of Paris and Florence to more obscure locations, more exclusive destinations that were not already thronging with droves of unimaginative Britons. Thus travel elitism was born.

North America soon became a fashionable destination in the nineteenth century, at the very time when the country was undergoing a domestic travel boom of its own after the privations of the Civil War. It lacked the attractions of the magnificent cities and ancient monuments of Europe, but a vast and fertile landscape on a scale unknown to Europeans took their place. Tourists began to home in on areas of natural beauty, such as the Niagara Falls in Canada, and, of course, hotels were built to accommodate this influx of new visitors.

'what separates the new hotel from just any hotel is the extra dimension of escapism that it offers its guests, namely the chance to experience, however briefly, a lifestyle that is glamorous, fashionable and exclusive.'

The new hotel

One defining characteristic of the new hotel, or at least the new hotel as discussed in this book, is its image of exclusivity. The target audience of design hotels are the very people who categorically do not want to join the exodus of the British abroad as they head towards the Costa del Sol or similar destinations for their annual holiday. It is snobbery, pure and simple, but the fact remains that it is this offer of exclusivity, the guarantee that a hotel is more imaginative and aspirational than others in its design, that marks out the territory of the new hotel. Also, as is discussed in greater depth regarding getaway hotels, location can play a key part, just as it did with the pioneers of the fashionable tour two centuries ago.

From tours to tourism

The rapid growth and diversity of tourism sparked another significant change. The popularization of foreign travel pioneered by Thomas Cook and others was both rapid and revolutionary. Railways and shipping lines had developed to such an extent during the nineteenth century that travelling abroad was becoming an increasingly viable option for many people, yet the practicalities of organizing foreign trips were still grossly complicated and certainly not geared to the budget traveller. The early tour operators of the mid-nineteenth century were thus something of a revelation. As more and more ordinary people started to view travel as a feasible part of their leisure agenda, there was suddenly more scope for a greater diversity of accommodation. The era of the modern hotel had arrived.

architectural
approaches

1

the exterior message

'The intention of the architect is to promote a sense of harmony between the hotel as an architectural statement and its existing natural habitat.'

Left and opposite *The Villa d'Este, Italy, stands regally amid ten acres of glorious gardens, surveying the shores of Lake Como, Italy. The Cardinal building, the main Renaissance villa, was built as a summer retreat for Cardinal Tolomeo Gallio in 1568. Occupied subsequently by a succession of aristocrats and rulers it was converted into a grand hotel in 1873 and now attracts guests seeking the splendours of bygone days.*

When analysing the exterior message of the new hotel it is important to consider the way in which its design and architecture relate to its environment. This is perhaps best illustrated by hotels that are set in areas of natural beauty.

Historically hotels that have been established in some of the outstanding beauty spots of the world have tended to impose their own contemporary architectural style on the surroundings, or else existing sites or buildings have been revamped to suit the chosen theme of the hotel. There are some particularly striking examples of this in Italy, including the Palazzo Sasso perched on the precipitous Amalfi coastline near Ravello and the Villa d'Este on the shores of Lake Como. The latter harmonizes with the other palatial buildings that line the lakeside but it embodies an approach very different from the contemporary search for architectural solutions. Modern hotel designers and architects tend to favour one of two approaches: they either create a hotel that draws heavily on elements of the indigenous architecture, so it blends seamlessly with its surroundings, or they favour the organic approach.

Organic design

Organic architecture is best defined, in terms of the new hotel at least, as that of a school of thought that considers the features of the natural environment that characterize the location of a building. At planning stage the building is

Left *The Absolut Ice Bar in the Ice Hotel, Sweden, is made from glistening blocks of ice and serves vodka in hollowed-out ice glasses. This is where the truly cool choose to chill out.*

Opposite page left *Couples can exchange marriage vows in the Ice Chapel, in front of guests in frozen pews draped with reindeer skins.*

Opposite page right *The hotel is the ultimate in organic architecture, a giant igloo built each winter from 30,000 tons of snow and 5,000 tons of crystal-clear ice from the nearby River Torne.*

conceived with considerations of terrain and landscape in mind, rather than with a determination to impose a stylized solution. The exterior message in this case is a sympathetic one based on a careful assessment and interpretation of the natural surroundings. The intention of the architect is to promote a sense of harmony between the hotel as an architectural statement and its existing natural habitat.

A landmark in the history of organic hotel architecture was the development of Sardinia's Costa Smeralda (the Emerald Coast) by the Aga Khan. The Porto Cervo, Capriccioli and Cala di Volpe areas of this 16- to 24-kilometre (10- to15-mile) stretch of feral coastline were targeted for tourist villas and apartments but strict guidelines were laid down to ensure that the natural beauty of the area remained unspoilt. The result is a collection of accommodations that have been designed with the surrounding villages' architecture in mind and finished in a palette of earthy colours that closely match the surrounding countryside.

This tradition of creating a sympathetic exterior message has continued through to the design of many new hotels, and with spectacular results. The Westin Regina Los Cabos in Mexico, for example, is a triumph of organic architecture: its rich, sun-baked colours complement the rusty earth of the surrounding coastline and the building's sensuous curve echoes the broad sweep of the beach. The sense of space created by the clean, sharp lines of the infinity pool and vibrant architectural sculptures ensures that the openness of the surrounding country is not wasted. Similarly, the Mövenpick Dead Sea resort in Amman seems, like the Cathar castles of southwestern France, to have sprouted out of the rocky terrain around it, so intimate is the relationship between design, materials and environment.

More dramatic still is the Hotel Explora in Patagonia (see p. 25). The remoteness of its location means that there are no other buildings in sight, making it imperative that the structure should coexist with, and more importantly not spoil, the soaring mountain peaks and dazzling lakes of this part of Chile. The low-rise design of the hotel means that it discreetly hugs the shoreline of the lake and was a careful attempt not to intrude on the stunning location. It could also be construed as a rather witty juxtaposition of forms, with the long, low, white building set against the backdrop of towering, snow-capped peaks on the horizon.

The distinctive organic style of the architect Frank Lloyd Wright was the inspiration behind the Canoe Bay resort in Wisconsin. Materials such as native cedar wood and stone were chosen to match the surrounding forest, as were certain interior features, such as a series of lamps crafted to resemble prairie flowers and plants. Even the shape of the building that houses the hotel's dining room is intended to mirror the geometry of the forest, as the horizontal 'branch' lines of its exterior contrast with the upright 'trunk' tower of the entrance. Inside, the high ceilings and large windows help to maintain a strong link with the hotel's natural setting.

The Ice Hotel in the freezing wilderness of Sweden's Arctic Circle must surely be the ultimate manifestation of organic design among contemporary hotels. As its name suggests, it is a hotel constructed entirely of ice and snow, whose guests sleep on beds of ice, swaddled in Arctic sleeping-bags. Every spring the structure melts away, then, as the weather turns cold again in winter, it is rebuilt for another season of intrepid tourists. Frozen Absolut vodka and excursions on snowmobiles stave off boredom, but for most visitors the sheer novelty of the place is enough.

Indigenous interiors

As has been mentioned, architects who are looking for ways to create a sense of harmony between the contemporary hotel and its natural environment also often draw inspiration from the indigenous architectural styles of that country or region. Aman Resorts are perhaps the pre-eminent proponents of this style, with a select number of hotels, typically in far-flung locations, that have adopted local building styles and materials in an effort to preserve the charm of the area.

Amanpuri in Phuket, Thailand, is probably one of the group's best-known forays into indigenous architecture, with the extraordinary temple design of its exterior and clean, warm interiors. This paved the way for a whole new approach to hotel design. The architect Ed Tuttle, apparently inspired by the temples of Ayutthya (the ancient capital of Thailand), managed to impart an authentic feel to this fantastical abstraction of traditional Thai architecture through minute attention to detail. Granite from local quarries and the rich, caramel colours of local woods are used in unusual and striking ways such as in the towering bedheads, which have since become a standard in contemporary hotel design.

Left *At the Hotel Bora Bora, Polynesia, nothing has been overlooked in the quest to provide an island idyll. Staying in authentic thatched huts or villas on stilts lapped by a turquoise lagoon, guests can live out their Gauguin fantasies in luxury and seclusion.*

Opposite *'The joy of the remote' is the motto of the Hotel Explora, Patagonia, and its quiet design cedes the limelight to its spectacular wilderness setting. Perched modestly beside the Rio Paine in the Torres del Paine National Park, it has a plain white exterior to match the encircling snowy mountains, and with its long, low layout is content to play second fiddle to their inimitable grandeur.*

to disturb the landscape with inappropriate and unfamiliar constructions. In the case of the Amandari in Bali, some of the rooms of the traditional thatched huts actually spill out into the garden area – the bathrooms, for instance, all have outdoor sunken marble baths nestling among the surrounding ferns and bamboo plants.

Modern makeovers

The Pousada Santa Maria de Flor da Rosa in Portugal (see p. 26) takes this approach one step further. This contemporary hotel successfully combines the traditional architecture of an ancient monastery fortress with austere modernism in a way that allows the two styles to interact rather than merely coexist. The main guest accommodation is housed in the stark, angular new wing, while the lobby, bar, restaurant and suites are all situated in the restored parts of the old church and monastery. To counterbalance the predominantly modern flavour of the interior design and to preserve a sense of place and history, the architect has also converted the original buildings that are not a part of the hotel and transformed them into a public museum. Pousada Santa Maria therefore constitutes a more radical and more complex approach to the issue of indigenous architecture than that of the Aman hotels. It is not just a case of incorporating echoes of the native architectural style into the design; instead the architect must graft a sympathetic modern appendage onto an historic buidling in a way that revitalizes and redefines the building as a whole.

Another new hotel that has successfully resurrected a remote fortress is the Devigarh Palace near Udaipur in India (see p. 27). As with the Pousada Santa Maria, original features, such as its fairytale palace windows and fabulous terraces, have been sensitively incorporated into what effectively amounts to a twenty-first-century makeover. Unlike the

Equally, ethnic fabrics, pictures and artefacts are used sparingly in order to give an authentic Thai flavour without compromising the signature Aman trappings of luxury and superlative comfort.

The Hotel Bora Bora is another typical example from the Aman portfolio. This quintessential huts-on-stilts hotel is situated on a small French Polynesian island north of Tahiti, and guests are ferried to the hotel reception in traditional native canoes. The 54 bungalows and *farés* (villas) that comprise the resort all have ceilings of *pandanus* (tropical palm-like plants) lashed to beams of Douglas fir, interiors of rattan and bamboo and are connected by solid lava-stone walkways. Many are literally poised over the water; others border pristine strips of beach and lush vegetation. The result is an architectural style that can deliver comfort and functionality while managing not

Opposite *At the Pousada Santa Maria de Flor da Rosa, Portugal, the hotel's architect had to fuse ancient and modern seamlessly. Ensuring that innovations like glass doors were as subtle and simple as possible was a key element of the scheme's success.*

Right *Originally an 18th-century fort, the Devigarh Palace near Udaipur, India, was the seat of a series of provincial rulers until 1997, when it was transformed into a tranquil, luxurious retreat for travellers. In the dining room pure white fabrics and beaten-silver bowls look fresh and contemporary, but are also timeless and thus perfect partners for the age-old architecture.*

Pousada, the Devigarh Palace has undergone mostly cosmetic rather than structural renovation. The inspiration behind much of the new interior owes a great deal to local craft and history, such as tapestries based on centuries-old Mogul motifs, but bedrooms, bathrooms and public areas have a distinctly contemporary, almost minimal, feel. There is no sign of cluttered ethnic furnishings and ornaments, just the calm, clean lines of white marble floors with vast, low beds and sofas or simple tabletops hewn from bone or semi-precious stone.

It is not only the independent operators who exploit the benefits of converting such grand and historic sites as the Devigarh Palace. The Inter-Continental hotel chain has maximized the potential of the Jacir Palace in Bethlehem by converting it into the city's first luxury hotel. The building was originally constructed in 1914 as a private residence and the ornate Franco-Moorish arches and windows that surround the courtyard, the gabled roof and domed basement presented the ideal canvas for a lavish, five-star hotel project.

Two new wings have been added to house the 250 guestrooms, and cosmetic work on the façade of the original building has revealed stonework that looks clean and fresh, harmonizing with the scrubbed, sympathetic pale stone of the new wings. An alfresco restaurant has been built on the roof, covered only by a slatted wood canopy. In short, the shell of the building has been cleverly manipulated to house the kind of upmarket hotel product that can trade well on the history and grandiose nature of the surroundings.

From cutting room to cutting edge

Of course, the juxtaposition of opposing styles is familiar territory in the world of contemporary hotel design and many of the landmarks in the history of the new hotel have cannibalized an existing building reformulating its style to serve a fresh purpose.

A prime example of this approach is André Balazs's Mercer hotel in New York (see p. 104). The architectural significance of the Mercer can only be properly understood in the context of its SoHo location. Historically SoHo was a deeply unfashionable, low-rent area of New York. In the wake of the Second World War the area's warehouses gradually fell into disrepair owing to the relocation of small manufacturing and storage industries out of New York into bigger factories in New Jersey, which inevitably resulted in depressed property prices. This created an opening in the 1960s and 1970s for aspiring artists to make use of all this available space and set up home and studio, establishing the style of loft-living that was to become so fashionable in the mid to late 1980s. And at this stage of SoHo's evolution, once the area had become synonymous with this exemplar of the aspirational lifestyle, the opportunity arose to exploit consumer demand by opening a design hotel modelled on the concept of loft-living.

Having identified the site on Mercer Street with a view to converting it into a cool, loft-style hotel, Balazs embarked on a design journey that took several years and several different designers to complete. Of course, during this time the public perception of cool continued to change, and the open-plan, almost spartan look of loft-living was succeeded by a new fashion for interiors that focused on luxury and comfort. This new trend became increasingly prevalent towards the end of the twentieth century and the result is that the seminal New York loft-style hotels, such as the Mercer and the SoHo Grand, actually bear little resemblance to the lofts that inspired them.

Both the Mercer and the Grand have redefined the image of the bare, open-plan design of the classic loft dwelling, substituting a new aesthetic that is tuned to the needs of a lifestyle hotel for the twenty-first century. The characteristic features of warehouse architecture are used to create an altogether different effect: high ceilings, large windows and timber floors maximize the available natural light and instil a sense of warmth in the interiors. The rooms at the Mercer, for example, are much smaller than would ordinarily be associated with a loft conversion but they retain a sense of volume despite the reduction in area and floor space.

The Gastwerk in Hamburg has also proved to be a very successful conversion of a former industrial property. In its previous life the hotel was a gasworks and the legacy of that existence is still evident in the high ceilings and substantial size of the guestrooms. The interior design utilizes the space well, focusing on warm natural colours and plenty of sunlight through the large windows. The result is a setting that is rustic in tone but is cleverly tempered with smooth modernism and the occasional flourish of exotic Eastern motifs. The restaurant fills an open-plan factory floor space, with plain red carpets, warm orange and brown upholstery, low lights and tall vases, which create an intimate mood in what could so easily be a very sterile space.

An international collaboration of architects – Australian Swaney Draper, Singapore's Terry Fripp and New York's Neil Bradford and Flaming Beacon – constitutes the distinguished team responsible for the acclaimed transformation of Melbourne's Lindrum from a turn-of-the-century warehouse into a design hotel for the new millennium. The design aims at the atmosphere of an updated gentleman's club, with deep leather chairs and billiard tables in the public areas complemented by polished guestroom interiors. The palette of colours is a smooth medley of subdued browns, charcoal and white, with high windows and easy chairs designed with comfort in mind. Lighting plays a key role in the ambience of the hotel, with the focus on warmly diffused table and standard lamps.

New Pioneers

Another Melbourne venture, the Prince, has proved one of the seminal landmarks in the development of that country's design hotel scene. Once a down-at-heel pub in a less than salubrious

Above Only the dimensions of the Gastwerk, Hamburg, give away its former identity as a gasworks. Now thick carpeting, subdued lighting, gleaming chrome and wooden furniture make for an atmosphere of studied calm.
Opposite A striking staircase of steel girders and steps studded with glass-bottle bottoms leads visitors from ground level to the main lobby and reception on the first floor of the SoHo Grand, New York. Bold, clanging, industrial, it is the designer's homage to SoHo's manufacturing heritage.

location, the Prince has spearheaded the gentrification of St Kilda and has stamped an indelible design statement on its art deco premises. Architect Allan Powell, who has described his role in the project as that of atmospheric strategist, has created a truly impressive modernist interior. The main aim of his strategy was to enhance the existing features of the building through careful design.

Judiciously placed furniture, such as the Marc Newson chairs in the lobby, is afforded extra impact by the clean, uncluttered lines of the rest of the interior. Other notable features are the extraordinary slumped glass bar in the cocktail lounge that has been sand-blasted to create a distinctive opaque finish; the plain, open space of the entrance lobby; and the economic, angular design of the guestrooms.

The use of restrained colours in the guestrooms creates a calming atmosphere that marries well with the plain symmetry of the low-slung platform beds, tidy storage units and bare white walls. Elsewhere in the hotel colour has been used effectively and provocatively to highlight key notes of the design. The walls of the Mink bar, for example, are bathed in a rich tobacco yellow; the booths are upholstered in crimson, with heavy, decadent drapes to match. The Soviet iconography that is scattered around the remainder of the bar completes the desired image of a decadent, almost illicit, drinking den.

However, the hotel's Circa restaurant has a contrasting sunny demeanour, thanks to the jaunty yellow upholstery of the chairs, the starched white tablecloths and flourishes of light wood (resembling slabs of driftwood that have been bleached and scoured by sun and sand). Strips of charcoal muslin that billow gently in the breeze artfully diffuse the light that streams in through the large windows. This is an environment that has been controlled not so much through the use of space (as elsewhere in the hotel) but through the use of colour, lighting and texture.

Preserving architectural integrity

Equally, the Schlosshotel Vier Jahreszeiten in Berlin represents another landmark in contemporary hotel design where an interesting building has been converted, modernized and imbued with a fresh design personality. Formerly a private aristocratic residence, the building itself has some architectural significance as a rare surviving example of late-Wilhelminian villa architecture, boasting many intricate original features, such as the delicately carved walls and ceilings. The conversion of this property, under the auspices of Karl Lagerfeld, has made full use of the potential for theatrical, larger-than-life interiors in order to create an updated version of the opulent townhouse residence for the modern traveller, while remaining faithful to some extent to the building's original identity. The association of Lagerfeld's name with the hotel intensifies this effect and creates the image of a luxurious urban retreat that is also linked to the worlds of fashion and design.

Andrée Putman also succeeded in making a seminal design statement when she coordinated the conversion of the Hotel im Wasserturm in Cologne (see p. 50). As influential as her work on Morgans in New York, the Wasserturm is an example of one of the first new hotels to use the novelty of its exterior and its prime location as a design message to the consumer. Its architectural form did not necessarily invite conversion into

Opposite Formerly known as the Prince of Wales, the Prince, Melbourne, is a stunning example of sensitive rejuvenation. Liberating the lobby of the erstwhile pub from paraphernalia and paint has let its structural beauty come to the fore, needing no adornment other than a Marc Newson chair.

a hotel, but innovative and imaginative design transformed much of the interior into a prototype bearing many of the elements that are now associated with the design hotel. These include the design-statement lobby, the signature bar and restaurant, inventive bathroom design and the use of familiar materials, such as stainless steel and ceramic tiles, in an interesting way.

Captive youth

It is therefore clear that a new style of conversion can be tailored to the evolving needs of a modern audience, while the existing attributes of the building itself are allowed to remain intact. But it is not necessarily the architectural attributes of a building that make it appropriate for conversion into a modern hotel; location also plays its part. Take the Standard in Los Angeles (see pp. 136–9), which used to be a residential home for the elderly – about as far removed as it is possible to get from its modern status as a funky hang-out for urbane urbanites.

Its location on Sunset Boulevard certainly helps lure the target audience, but what is interesting about the Standard is not just the design but also the price, the crowd and the transient appeal of the way in which it has been converted. It

'it is not necessarily the architectural attributes of a building that make it appropriate for conversion into a modern hotel; location also plays its part.'

has been constructed almost like a film set to strike a chord with a fashionable crowd but, like fashion, it has a kind of disposable quality about it. The use of shagpile carpets on the floor and walls of the lobby, the metallic 1970s light shades and soft, round forms of the seating prevent any sense that the interior will never be redesigned – this is a style that has been conceived with the zeitgeist in mind. There are no huge chunks of marble or limestone, say, which might imply a lasting design statement; instead the design plays on the lounge-type, retro style personified by cult figures such as Austin Powers. Naturally, then, the shelf life of this design is dictated by how long that particular style retains its cultural currency before becoming effectively obsolete and in need of renewal.

On the other side of the world, a similar play for the youth dollar will be underway in Sydney's Lotel. This hotel has been revamped by new owners, who enlisted the design counsel of Iain Halliday for the project. He is renowned as the man who

worked on the highly successful image of the Kirketon, but Lotel is a more modest venture, combining affordability with a very specific design manifesto that reinvents the French *pension* with considerable panache. Expansive glass doors at either end of the ground floor of the property showcase the frenetic café, bar and restaurant. The Le Corbusier stools at the entrance establish the hotel's intention to appeal to a resolutely design-literate punter and this theme continues throughout the remaining interior spaces, which use French blue tiles and plenty of bright white space to maximum effect.

The emergence of hotels such as Lotel or the Prince of Wales is a good indication of the burgeoning demand for design hotels among the elusive youth market. Like the Standard in Los Angeles, for example, these hotels are offering a finely tuned design product at very affordable prices. Certain districts of certain cities then become desirable youth markets for the design hotel operator. The St Kilda neighbourhood of Melbourne (where the Prince is to be found), TriBeCa in New York (the location of the eponymous TriBeCa Grand) and Shoreditch (London's coolest enclave of bohemia and the chosen site of the Shoreditch hotel) are all notable examples.

Home from home

Perhaps the most advanced and certainly the most flamboyant example of a design hotel that specifically targets the youth market is Jonathan Morr's Townhouse (see pp. 140–45) in Miami's funky South Beach neighbourhood. The interior design, courtesy of ascendant young talent India Mahdavi, works to

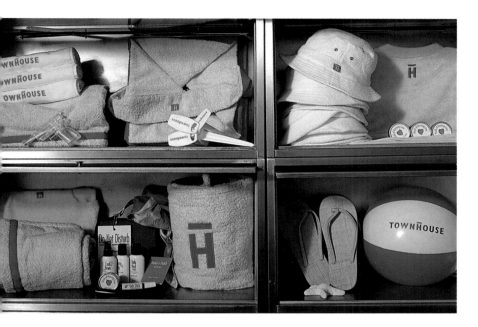 

Morr's brief that Townhouse should be a fresh, happy, fun place to stay. There is also a great emphasis on affordability, or more specifically affordable style, in the hotel's marketing and publicity literature. This is a hotel that has been designed as a user-friendly, inexpensive destination that caters to the city's growing population of design-conscious young professionals who want to spend some quality lounging time in stimulating surroundings.

The design is geared to complement this kind of easy-going lifestyle – in fact, the two are inextricably linked. Each of the guestrooms, for instance, is equipped with a large L-shaped sofa that doubles as an extra bed to accommodate a third overnight guest (at no extra charge). The suggestion is that guests can just relax and treat this hotel like an extension of their own home.

Townhouse is a carefully thought-out project and is successful not least because it has a very focused idea of its target audience. The Bond St Lounge – the hotel's restaurant and sibling of the highly successful Manhattan establishment of the same name – is further proof that Jonathan Morr has studied the market closely before committing to the concrete considerations of the design and marketing of his product.

Banishing the clichés

The Hotel Pelirocco in Brighton, England, is another example of a design hotel that has been tailored to suit the needs and pockets of a younger and, from the design viewpoint at least, more demanding clientele. The young operators were already tuned into the scene in Brighton, having spent a great deal of their time visiting the town during breaks from London. They saw a gap in a market that is ostensibly dominated by tatty boarding-houses and tacky bed-and-breakfast establishments, and decided to corner the young bucks with a design hotel that offered fashionable, funky accommodation at guesthouse prices.

The idea was picked up by several artists and designers such as Jamie Reid and Nicola Bowery, as well as by some unexpected figures from the music industry, such as Bobby Gillespie (lead singer of rock band Primal Scream) and local record labels Asian Dub Foundation and Skint. Each room has been designed by a different team and they all have a distinctive, highly idiosyncratic flavour. There is the Modrophenia room, for instance, whose target duvets and

Lambretta mirrors are a homage to the resurgent mod culture of the 1960s, and the PlayStation room, which offers game consoles and a late-check-out option. The Pussy room has a giant picture of the Manhattan skyline covering an entire wall, while Betty's Boudoir is an unrestrained homage to the 1950s American porn queen.

The Pelirocco captures the spirit of an ascendant market of sophisticated, irreverent young punters who are rejecting the cliché of seaside hotels and sleepy resorts. Instead they are looking for a place to stay that recognizes and is eager to accommodate their own tastes and lifestyle aspirations. It is hard not to see the appeal of picking up the boxing-glove-shaped telephone in the Muhammad Ali room and ordering some room service.

Master of reinvention

Location was one of the primary considerations behind the Great Eastern Hotel, since it can lay claim to the undoubted distinction of being the first design hotel in the City of London. It is housed within the walls of a grand Victorian railway hotel that had slipped into a state of disrepair; this makes it an unusual example of a contemporary hotel conversion, since the building's previous incarnation was also that of a hotel. Nevertheless it is a significant one, which plays cleverly on the historical resonance it has inherited from its predecessor while managing to assert its identity as a new hotel.

The Great Eastern Hotel is an attempt to reinvent and remodel the concept of the Victorian railway-station hotel, with all the attendant pomp and ceremony, and serve it up in a form that is both appropriate and palatable to a modern audience. Jonathan Manser's architecture and Terence Conran's interior

design have emblazoned a sense of style and glamour on the premises that, although firmly rooted at the cutting edge of twenty-first-century taste, also recalls the former identity of the hotel. The soaring lobby and the hard-edged modernity of the atrium ceiling place it squarely in the new millenium but the almost sentimental design motifs of the hotel's Aurora restaurant, for instance, with its stained-glass dome and murals of frolicking nymphs, hark back to a bygone era.

Both the original architect, Charles Barry, who drafted the plans to which the hotel was built in 1884, and Colonel W. Edis, who expanded the hotel at the beginning of the twentieth century, opted for a lavish, almost ostentatious design. Similarly, Conran's approach hints at an opulent, lavish lifestyle and a sense of exclusivity intended to lure the target audience of moneyed suits and a high-rolling younger clientele. Even the furniture is upholstered in smart suit fabrics, while the immaculately bare surfaces of the bedrooms are preserved by discreet computer and modem powerpoints that are sunk into the desktop. The message is quite clearly linked to the hotel's location and is equally clearly stamped on every inch of its design: this is a modern lifestyle space where the hardworking executive can unwind in grand style.

Opposite *The awesome Gothic façade of the Great Eastern Hotel, London, would be recognizable to its Victorian architects but once inside they would be fast-forwarded to the ultimate in twenty-first-century style. Though keeping faith with the spirit of the golden age of railway travel by restoring or replicating period details, the designers also introduced an utterly contemporary vision, blending the best of old and new so that the very latest technologies dovetail with their august surroundings.*

signage and branding

making the right impression

'It is vital from the outset that the customer receives the right message about the hotel, and this process begins even before he or she checks in.'

The new hotel is not a brand or even a design; rather, it is an experience and a challenge. In some respects the hotel industry is the ultimate service industry. But, linked with service, the new hotel has to meet the challenge of recognizing its market, its clients and its parameters. In real-estate terms, the hotel is about three issues: location, location, location. Add to this convenience, price, sex appeal and amenities offered, and the result can be compared to the bespoke tailor offering a made-to-measure service: the hotel must be perceived as being completely customer-oriented. It is vital from the outset that the customer receives the right message about the hotel, and this process begins even before he or she checks in.

First impressions

Seeing any building for the first time automatically leads to some degree of speculation as to what it might be like inside, what kind of people go there, and so on. When it comes to hotels, this is more than just idle speculation. The building itself provides a valuable first impression, one that can be finely tuned and carefully targeted to appeal to a certain audience.

A wide range of considerations must be taken into account if the exterior message is to be conveyed effectively. The various elements of the external design and architecture of a hotel can be shaped, refined, altered or reconstructed to deliver a coherent message to its target market. Signage, exterior lighting, the entrance doors and even the door staff can all have significant impact.

Name, please

A hotel's sign and its branding both serve a common purpose: to express and advertise that establishment's identity. As a result, an analysis of hotel signage inevitably leads to discussion of branding issues, and vice versa, but the two should not be confused. Signage is the physical or graphic representation that names, locates and identifies a hotel; it can be written or illustrated, it can even be a three-dimensional sculpture. But a sign can also convey more information than that, when it points towards a common culture of design and service. That is when it becomes a brand.

The primary function of the sign is to encapsulate the identity of the hotel as clearly and succinctly as possible. The sign is not just a part of the exterior message of a hotel – that is, the board that swings in the wind above the door – but is also used in printed form in brochures, advertising and so on. The onus on the designer, then, is to hit upon the right image for the hotel, an image that says to the target audience this is the place for you, this is what you are looking for. This is a message that comes in all shapes and sizes.

Opposite *The sign outside the Avalon, Beverly Hills, communicates the hotel's character brilliantly. Lower-case letters in different typefaces, stuck on a golfball surface, announce a playful penchant for the incongruous and the goofy.*

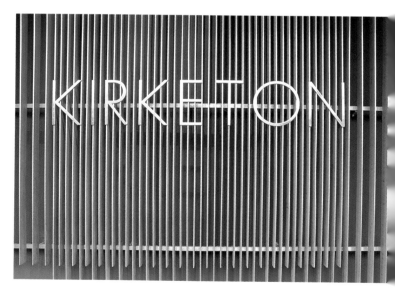

Above left *The distinctive cursive script chosen for Blakes, London, reflects the bold, historical influences of its interior aesthetic.*

Above right *A single sans-serif letter, needing no flourishes, speaks volumes about the W hotel chain's restrained style ethos.*

Above *Reading between the lines, anyone approaching the Kirketon, Sydney, can sense from its sign that a pared-down, stark look is the dominant theme.*

Left *Neon is not normally associated with subtlety, but the neon-green name of the Savoy, London, spells classic style and sophistication.*

The cliché of Las Vegas-style flashing neon signs that reached its zenith in the 1960s and 1970s belongs to a different universe from that of the discerning market (labelled AB1 consumers). It represents a brash, garish appeal aimed squarely at those who do not have a specific destination in mind and need to be strongly reminded of where they are and what they are looking for. This is altogether different from the low-key chic of London's Berkeley, for example. The type of discreet signage it wears is intended for those who know where they are going and simply need confirmation that they are in the right place. But it is also saying something else: this is a hotel that does not need to resort to meretricious show or flaunt its goods; it has class.

Discretion guaranteed

At the beginning of the twenty-first century the discreet sign is becoming increasingly commonplace. Tastes have evolved and the worldly customers of the new hotel are a more sophisticated group. It has become more fashionable, more cutting-edge, to make signage as understated as possible, interestingly even in the case of hotels that are part of a worldwide chain. Signs like those of the Starwood Hotel Group's W hotels imply a uniquely sophisticated experience, despite the existence of dozens of other editions. In this instance the sign acts as a hallmark, a guarantee that certain standards will be maintained. Similarly, hip hotels like the Avalon in Beverly Hills (see p. 39) or the Medusa in Sydney (see pp. 172–75) draw inspiration from the world of fashion to produce signs that have enough cultural currency to lure bright young consumers with the promise of cool and like-minded punters.

Other signs, like that of One Aldwych in London (see p. 54), communicate a deliberately confused message. The passer-by will be left wondering if this is a bank or an office rather than a hotel. This tactic takes the concept of understated signage a step further into territory that could justifiably be called 'ambiguous signage'. In this case the exterior message states: if you have to ask, don't bother coming in. The ambiguous sign intimidates those who are not sure, who do not already know this is a destination hotel, by prolonging the uncertainty. Equally, for those who are actually staying at the hotel, the ambiguous sign instils a sense of superiority, a sense that they belong to a group that is set apart from the crowd.

Similarly, the sign outside the Standard in Los Angeles (see p.37), which hangs upside down, is making a strong statement about the kind of place it is advertising. Customers are duly informed that this is a hotel where nothing is as it seems, thereby confirming that the apparently trite and kitsch interior is in fact a deliberate and frightfully fashionable post-modern joke intended to amuse and delight an equally fashionable crowd.

Making a statement

A sign can also become a landmark in its own right when the hotel itself is not immediately obvious – perhaps it is set back from the street or obscured by other buildings and trees. One example of this is the internationally recognized sign that marks the way to the Savoy, which is neatly tucked behind the Strand in London. The subtle use of green neon gives the sign of the hotel itself – as well as the adjacent Savoy Theatre, which also helps to locate the hotel – a restrained eye-catching quality. The neon signage of the Savoy Theatre also makes it conspicuous enough to be discernible at a distance from which the hotel itself may not yet be visible. In this case it is the sign rather than the hotel that becomes the landmark.

However, when the architecture of the hotel is out of the ordinary, the physical presence of the building tends to be the recognized landmark and negates any need for a sign. In such

'when the architecture of the hotel is out of the ordinary, the physical presence of the building tends to be the recognized landmark and negates any need for a sign.'

cases, the building itself becomes the sign. The Burj al Arab in Dubai (see p. 42), for example, emits a proud exterior message. The world's tallest hotel, its glittering mass of glass, steel and gold leaf makes it easily the most extraordinary feature of the space-age skyline of Jumeirah Beach, next to which any kind of subtle signage would appear absurd.

A similar example would be the extraordinary New York, New York (see p. 44) in Las Vegas whose 2,000-plus rooms are housed in a structure that has been designed to replicate the Manhattan skyline. Perhaps more excessive still is the roller-coaster that whips its cargo of screaming guests around the front of the hotel's casino at nearly 110 kilometres (70 miles) per hour. It is hard not to regard this edifice as a phenomenal expression of over-the-top Americana but there is no doubting the potency of its exterior message: this is one of the wonders of the neon-bathed world that is Las Vegas. Thrill-seekers are welcome.

Aldo Rossi's Il Palazzo in Fukuoka, south-west Japan, is an early example of a new hotel that issued a strong signage statement through its architecture. The exterior is a post-modern temple of brick masonry and expressed-steel lintels that reinvents classical orders and, in so doing, indicates to the potential customer that this is an intelligently designed hotel that can challenge the architecturally aware guest.

Signage versus branding

Perhaps the best way to illustrate the link between signage and branding would be to reconsider the sign at the Avalon in Beverly Hills alongside some of the hotel's marketing literature. The same signage appears on the front of the brochure, accompanied by the logo, which in turn appears throughout the hotel in various forms. This is an example of a stand-alone brand, which is the first, most basic extension of the signage principle: the hotel is given a stronger sense of identity and strengthens its message to the consumer through the use of visual branding. Like signage, hotel branding gives clues about the experience that awaits the customer by hinting at such diverse issues as fashion and lifestyle, status, price and market, design and standards of facilities and service. Of course, another parallel between signage and branding is that both can achieve various levels of subtlety.

The sign at the Avalon merely intimates that the potential customer can expect a design- and fashion-conscious environment. This low-key style of branding is supported, in this case, by the cool modernism of the interior design and premises that were originally brought to life in 1949 by Alvin Lustig. A palette of clean white walls, natural light flooding through large windows and funky Barbarella furniture assures the clientele that they have not been misled.

The lifestyle message

A more sophisticated version of this principle of seductive lifestyle marketing is the website of the Hard Rock hotel and casino in Las Vegas. The potential customer is assaulted by cartoons of lithe models in bikinis and the opportunity for instant access to a 24-hour webcam that monitors the resort's swimming pool, not to mention trendy graphics and the promise of live music and high-stakes gambling. The lifestyle message of this hotel is patently clear: fun, fun, fun. Pictures of gaming tables adorned with a martini and cigar hint at a kind of decadent, James Bond lifestyle that seems to be confirmed by the advertisement for the hotel's nightclub,

Above *A shimmering sail-shaped skyscraper soaring 321 metres above the Arabian Gulf, the Burj al Arab, Dubai, is an architectural and engineering phenomenon. A global landmark in its own right, it needs no sign to proclaim its presence.*

Opposite *The Hotel Arts, Barcelona, is similarly recognizable from its amazing construction alone. Apart from being the city's tallest building, it stands out like a beacon because of its white scaffold-like exterior, which arms the tower against the wind. A vast fish sculpture by Frank Gehry floats at its foot.*

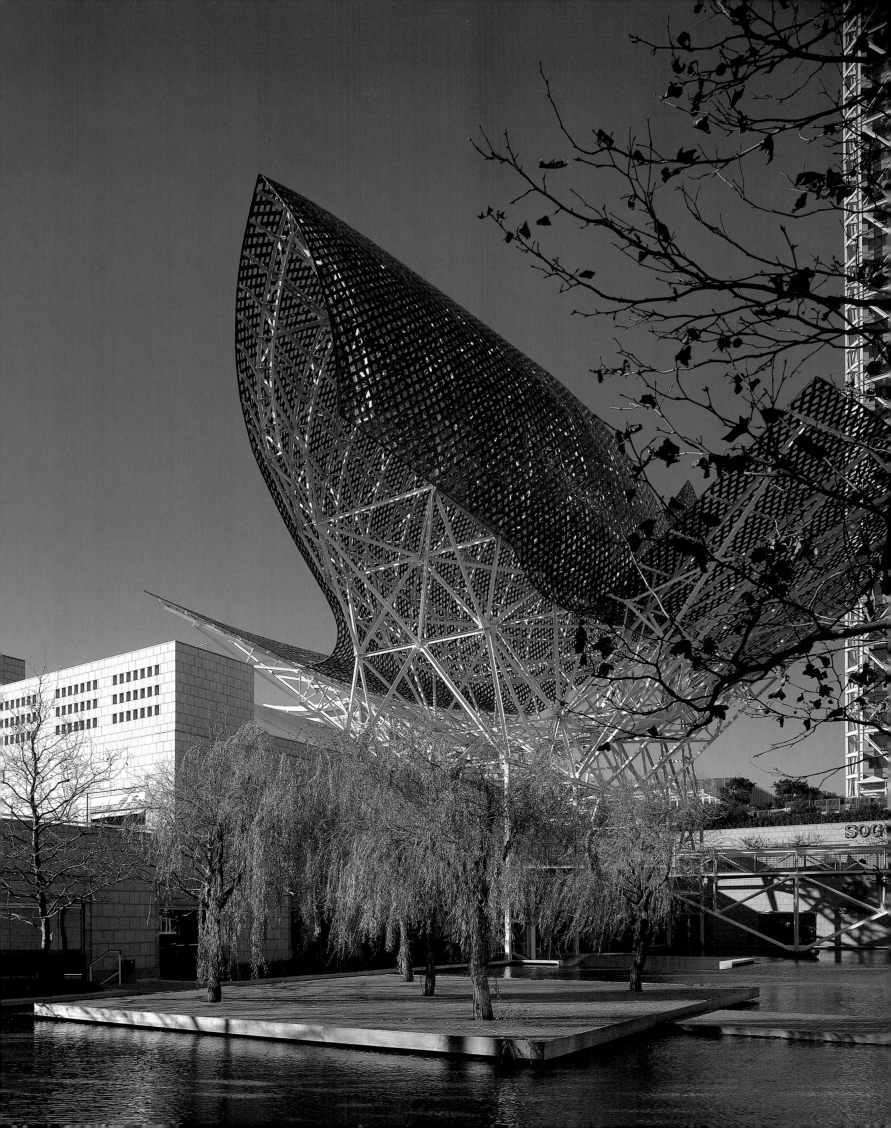

Baby's. Designed by Sean MacPherson, it comprises an enticing picture of a Baywatch-style babe behind a bar stocked with glittering bottles of spirits.

Pictures of the rooms are also posted on the website, revealing a kind of rock 'n' roll glamour that would not look out of place in a magazine fashion spread, while the cool brick-and-stone lines of the Rockspa promise a quiet retreat for when the party is over. There are also postcards that can be emailed to friends, depicting beautiful people lounging in the spa and an archetypal rock dude watching, drink in hand, as his groupies gyrate around the room. In short, the website is making a bold and unequivocal statement about the kind of lifestyle that the Hard Rock brand is promising its clientele: namely the opportunity to assume the fantasy persona of a rock star, albeit for a limited period.

David versus Goliath

Design hotels do not tend to use branding in the same way that a multinational chain of hotels may use it. Mainstream hotel brands like Inter-Continental, Marriott or Le Meridien, for example, use advertising and promotional activity to draw attention to loyalty schemes, business and fitness centres and other facilities that might suit the needs of their target audience. The brand name therefore becomes a guarantee that these extra options will be available. Irrespective of a person's location in the world, as long as he or she sees the Marriott brand name, for instance, there will be no doubt that the attendant facilities are on site, along with the bespoke Marriott service and experience.

But design hotels opt for a more subtle strategy, a strategy that is specifically aimed at a discerning section of the market, as opposed to the mass appeal of the big brand names. Hotels designed by gurus like Ian Schrager or Anouska Hempel, which are destinations for a more elite target audience, achieve their brand identity via a more tortuous route. These properties are not branded in a mainstream way using logos, brand names and common design templates that state in unequivocal terms: this is an Ian Schrager hotel. Instead a Schrager hotel can be recognized through common

features – design or otherwise – that have been brought to the potential customer's attention through articles in the ordinary media and the fashion and lifestyle press. Design hotels rely on the impact of the property itself, combined with considerable PR spend, to generate media attention and public awareness. Thus the brand becomes inextricable from the design, and the work of a particular designer constitutes the commonality rather than the blatant stamp of a multinational group.

The design message

Consider the example of the two Blakes hotels. Ostensibly they are different townhouse hotels – one in London (see pp. 46–7) and the other in Amsterdam – but they both bear the discreet brand of Anouska Hempel's design. True, they both have the same name and are linked in this way, but there is also a finer common thread that binds them. The fact that the Hempel and Blakes in London had already firmly rooted the name and work of this designer in the public consciousness meant that certain expectations were attached to the opening of Blakes in Amsterdam. What can be construed as trademark Hempel

> 'design hotels opt for a more subtle strategy, a strategy that is specifically aimed at a discerning section of the market, as opposed to the mass appeal of the big brand names'

style – an eclectic range of ethnic antiques, cosmopolitan design influences and rich colours – was expected when it was announced that a new Hempel-designed hotel was due to open in the Netherlands.

Naturally the influences for both Blakes hotels were different but the characteristics of Hempel's work are discernible in both, therefore meeting consumer expectations and, in this sense, perpetuating the brand. Theatrical design, opulent colours and lavish fabrics mingled with antique exotica characterize the bedrooms in London and Amsterdam; the penchant for symmetrical arrangements of neatly potted plants, exposed brickwork and imposing umbrellas are the hallmarks of both courtyards. This is the subtlest form of branding: playing on consumer aspirations by using superb design to create destinations that are linked, in the media – and consequently in the mind of the consumer – with a desirable image or lifestyle.

Small is beautiful

Associations of luxury and exclusivity that might be generated by the brand name of a group of hotels often help to attract the attention of a more sophisticated audience with a greater spending power. The Small Hotel Company, for instance, is a name that implies quality derived from some kind of rigorous selection procedure. The company specializes in boutique hotels – like Le Priori in Quebec, Canada, and hideaway resorts, such as the Vahine Island Resort in French Polynesia – that thrive on their word-of-mouth image. The goal of brands like the Small Hotel Company is to foster a clientele who desire to avoid mass-marketed resorts and who wish to feel that they are part of a more elite group of discerning travellers who truly appreciate quality. In this context, the label of small hotel is an instant attraction and becomes an integral part of the branding exercise.

Location, location, location

The choice of location for a hotel can also play its part in the overall branding. Some hotel chains, for example Aman Resorts, use the geographical locations of their hotels as a part of their branding exercise. Each hotel is named according to its location, such as Amangani in Wyoming (see pp. 48–9), which takes the second half of its name from an indigenous Native North American language. This creates a superficial connection between the hotel and its surroundings, which is further endorsed by the layout and design of the establishment. Amangani's swimming pool overlooking the extraordinary vista of surrounding desert and mountains is a good example. This is a hotel that is clearly not based in a convenient or particularly accessible location, and every aspect of its design is intended to emphasize its remote setting. In short, it is positioning itself as a destination hotel.

this issue does not apply to the select few hotels that use the stamp of an individual designer's work as a branding tool, as previously discussed. It does apply to the mainstream of hotel brands, which, when they work, are an effective shorthand endorsement of what each group of hotels can offer, but, when unsuccessful, can fast become a liability.

Finding yourself

When the American real-estate giant The Blackstone Group swooped in and acquired the Savoy hotel group in May 1998 there was a great deal of speculation as to whether these well-established brands would be handled and developed responsibly and sensitively. As it turns out, Blackstone has provided a textbook example of how a well-established, prestigious brand can be astutely updated and streamlined to compete in the modern marketplace.

The Savoy, the Berkeley, Claridge's and the Connaught are four of London's best-known hotels and among the most respected properties in the world, which means that the issue of refining and developing each hotel under the new Blackstone umbrella was a delicate one. John Ceriale, managing director of Blackstone, believes the individual identity of each of these hotels is key to their success and should not be swamped by heavy-handed branding.

'We look at this as the Savoy company and within this company are four very strong brands – the Berkeley, the Connaught, Claridge's and the Savoy – and we are interested in keeping those brands strong. When you start doing some research you realize that many people do not know that Claridge's is a Savoy hotel, because Claridge's, just like the Connaught, is a brand that stands by itself. We don't want to change that; we just want to deliver services that benefit all the hotels but are invisible to the customer, such as a centralized reservations system or centralized sales and marketing and human resources operations.'

The important point in this instance is that the Blackstone Group is able to apply a common standard of service to all its hotels in a way that is not immediately noticeable to the consumer. In a sense the illusion of an independent, family-run property is maintained in a hotel such as Claridge's, with no visible signs of chain marketing in evidence, but the twenty-first-century corporate makeover has in fact been applied. Ceriale is convinced that this more subtle form of branding will continue to attract the loyalty of the hotels' traditionally elite international clientele.

The opposite end of the spectrum would be a brand such as Posthouse Forte. Mass-market business travellers will tend to stay at the Posthouse Forte in Birmingham, say, not because it is worth the trip to Birmingham to stay there but because they happen already to be there on business and need somewhere to stay. The Posthouse Forte brand guarantees availability through the sheer number of its branches, which in turn guarantee the same ease of use, comfortable accommodation and homogenized interiors. In this instance the uniqueness of the location could not be further removed from the appeal of the brand.

Nevertheless uniformity and commonality are essential to the success of any brand, irrespective of its target audience. There is still a balance to be struck: namely the balance between the integrity and consistency of the brand and the individual identity of each property within that brand. Clearly

Above and left Branding is subliminal and highly sophisticated at Blakes, London. Logos and identikit facilities have no place here; rather, the hotel's uniqueness is evident everywhere in its design credo. Each of the 50 guest suites is delightfully different but all bear the stamp of owner and designer Anouska Hempel, who travelled the globe in search of fascinating antiques and artefacts. A Biedermeier table, a Thai chest of drawers, a Turkish rug, mingle with sumptuous fabrics to create in each room a cosmopolitan cocoon of consummate comfort.

'It is not necessary for every hotel in our group to have the same amenities, the same format or the same interior design. Take shoe-shining as an example: in each of the hotels you can kick off your shoes at night and they come back shined, and that is the service standard. But the presentation doesn't necessarily have to be the same – they may come back wrapped, in a bag or as you left them, depending on which hotel you are in. It's not like a Four Seasons hotel, for example, which offers the same five-star experience wherever you are in the world. Of course, there is nothing wrong in that, as it means you know you can never go wrong staying in a Four Seasons hotel. But you might find that there are other hotels that suit your own style a little better.'

Targeting the customer

Blackstone is interested in actively seeking out the top-end consumer who is more likely to be seduced by the non-chain, luxury-hotel experience. Since acquiring the Savoy group Blackstone has sought to remedy what it perceived as the under-marketing of these hotels by applying a more active marketing strategy. In order to do this Ceriale feels that it is necessary to build a tighter, more defined picture of customers and the kind of lifestyle to which they might aspire.

'As far as the Savoy group of hotels is concerned, we have a huge amount of respect for those properties, for the brand and for where they are positioned. We look at these hotels as almost a luxury-brand company, just like Louis Vuitton, for example, or Vendôme, which owns Cartier, Mont Blanc, Chloé and Purdey. Just as those products are a collection of luxury brands, we look at these hotels as a collection of luxury brands as well. We have established a number of marketing relationships with other luxury brands, such as Concorde, American Airlines Platinum scheme, Rolls Royce, Sony (in particular Sony Classical Music) and Hermès.'

By forging strong links with established luxury brands Blackstone is strengthening the image of its hotels and making them more available to the chosen target audience. Consumers who fit the profile of Rolls Royce drivers or those who shop at Hermès are far more likely to be interested in classical music or opera than any other consumer group. Therefore the fit has to be exact and the aspirations of the target audience must be taken into account at every stage. Connections with products such as Concorde and American Airlines Platinum scheme also help to position the hotels at the top end of the business market, which is clearly another crucial aspect of the twenty-first-century travel market.

Maximizing potential

As Ceriale explains, the new hotel has a unique advantage over other kinds of businesses when it comes to gathering information on its customers. 'One of the things we have in our company that a lot of other businesses do not is a

comprehensive customer database. We are in a situation, unlike a retailer for example, where a customer gives his or her name, address and even an email address when he or she checks in and registers. We have been able to set up a good website and we are no longer part of the Leading Hotels of the World group because we now feel that our hotel group is strong enough to stand alone.'

The approach that Blackstone has adopted to the Savoy group of hotels demonstrates that branding can be highly effective without compromising the individual character and reputation of each of the hotels. In fact it is that sense of individual charm that becomes each hotel's unique selling point, in the same way that the work of a particular designer can be used as a branding and marketing tool. However, the disadvantage of this kind of approach is that it can become very difficult to enlarge the brand, since there are so few hotels that would fit the image of the group and those that do exist are often privately owned and practically impossible to acquire.

Ceriale is aware of this problem, although he feels that there are also ways of maximizing the potential of the existing brand while waiting for what he describes as a rare opportunity to expand the portfolio of the Savoy group.

'Opportunities to buy a hotel that fits this group of hotels do not come very often and when suitable properties do come on the market they are not inexpensive. This makes it very difficult to increase the size of this company. What we want to do is to find a hotel that fits the group: then we can figure out how to purchase it in a way that would make good economic sense for our investors. But there are probably only about ten hotels in the world that could support the kind of service that we are offering in the Savoy group; in other words, hotels that have an average rate high enough to allow us to deliver good service. So there are hotels that could be Savoy hotels, such as the Crillon in Paris, but breaking these hotels loose is not easy. It took a hundred years to break the Savoy loose and a lot of these other hotels are in families as well.'

Exterior lighting

When considering the hotel as a physical landmark, lighting is an important way of communicating a message to the consumer. The primary purpose of bold neon signage has already been discussed (see pp.40–41) but this kind of mass-market branding can also have a secondary function as a form of exterior lighting. On a basic level the garish neon sign of Caesar's Palace in Las Vegas, for example, is an obvious attention-grabbing device and represents a common form of exterior lighting.

Compare this to the St Martins Lane hotel in London, however, and the range of effects that can be achieved through lighting becomes apparent. The rather ordinary exterior of St Martins Lane does little to distinguish it from the surrounding office blocks and administrative buildings of Covent Garden, especially when seen at night. In cases like this the issue of lighting therefore becomes an important consideration for the designer whose task it is to identify the building properly as a destination design hotel. The desired result is achieved at St Martins Lane through an indirect form of exterior lighting whereby the different colours of light radiating from the guestrooms forms a mosaic of light across the façade of the hotel.

The Hotel Saratz in Switzerland's exclusive St Moritz resort uses the same effect but for a slightly different reason. This hotel is a contemporary restoration of what was a very traditional hostelry, so it was the need to reposition this property subtly as a modern design hotel that makes this form of lighting fundamental to the overall exterior message. The impression created by the night-time façade of the Hotel Saratz is that of a contemporary destination hotel that has eschewed conventional techniques of exterior lighting in favour of a more stylized approach.

Although the function of exterior lighting as a means of identifying a hotel is of crucial importance, its principal function is best described as cosmetic. Consider the nature of a hotel: it is a business that needs to operate around the clock, seven days a week. Add to that the role of the exterior message in terms of a hotel's business success (that is, it stands less chance of attracting customers if it does not look good) and the aesthetic importance of lighting is obvious. The design hotel can be compared to a fashion-conscious, meticulous dresser for whom only the best fabrics and the most expensive labels will possibly do. It follows, then, that extra-special care should be taken over the evening makeover, the point at which the cosmetics are applied before heading out into the public gaze. Thus the exterior lighting of the design hotel is vital to the impression it makes.

Take the example of the Hotel Kyocera in Kagoshima, south-west Japan. The atrium design works well during the day, when the available natural light is used to good effect, but it runs the risk of appearing inert and soulless when seen at night. This potential pitfall is overcome through intelligent use of lighting: the light from the exposed balcony corridors inside the hotel is used to emanate a warm, welcoming glow from the core of the building. Similarly, Andrée Putman's impressive Hotel im Wasserturm in Cologne benefits from carefully positioned spotlighting that softens what would otherwise be a foreboding, almost gothic, night-time exterior.

Far left *At night The Hôtel, Lucerne, presents a tantalizing preview of what lies within, as giant stills from films are projected onto guestroom ceilings, transforming the frontage into a magical multicoloured mosaic.*

Above left *After dark, skilful uplighting illuminates the chalk-white face of Hotel Dorint am Gendarmenmarkt, Berlin, while the entrance is ingeniously designed to resemble a photographer's lightbox.*

Left *Unlit at night, the Wasserturm, Cologne, could look offputtingly like the redundant nineteenth-century watertower it once was. In its present-day incarnation as a luxury hotel, exterior spotlights supply a welcoming glow that woos visitors inside to discover elegant guestrooms and a glass-enclosed rooftop restaurant with stunning views over the city.*

making an entrance

3

first contact

'As with other aspects of the exterior message, the design of the entrance tends to make a strong statement about the hotel.'

The exterior message of the new hotel can be broken down into key contributing parts. The function of signage and branding, architecture and lighting have all been discussed at length but there is another important and often neglected opportunity to make a statement about a hotel, namely in the design of the entrance itself.

The entrance doors of a hotel are usually the most intricate feature of its exterior design and, as such, can often be the most eloquent mouthpiece for the hotel as a whole. It is common among new hotels for the entrance to be designed in such a way that the customer is given a foretaste, almost like an advance warning, of what the design of the rest of the hotel is going to be like. As with other aspects of the exterior message, the design of the entrance tends to make a strong statement about the hotel. There is none of the subtlety that might characterize the finer points of the interior design; the entrance is tackling the broader questions that are in the mind of the potential customer: is it modern or classic, a design

Left By day the exterior of One Aldwych, London, has all the gravitas befitting one of the city's most elegant Edwardian buildings, designed in 1907 for The Morning Post. By night inspired lighting makes the glass doors and mica flakes in the Norwegian granite sparkle, suggesting glittering celebrations within.
Opposite St Martins Lane, London, used to be the Lumière cinema. The daunting revolving door seems designed for the larger-than-life film stars it often ushers in, rather than mere mortals.

hotel or a comfortable, more family-oriented place? In the same way that signage tries to appeal to a target audience, the design of the entrance can also act as a filter for the kinds of customers the hotel is trying to attract. A more open, less stylized, design might foster an accessible image that implies people are welcome to come in for a closer look, but the chic, expensive-looking entrance can convey the definite impression that this is a strictly private hotel.

In what ways, then, can the entrance become a visual précis of the style of a hotel? The Hôtel Costes in Paris epitomizes the small boutique hotel with a discreet entrance: it stands at the end of a rather unprepossessing corridor leading from the rue Faubourg St-Honoré that opens up into a fashionable, stylish set of rooms and courtyard. This entrance is not a meretricious come-on but one that coyly conceals rather than flaunts its charms. The message is purely and simply a statement of understatement. A glitzy entrance with plenty of ornate and elaborate design features would never be able to convey the same quiet confidence, and the implicit message is that this hotel does not need to make a huge effort to attract customers.

Making a statement

However, a bold statement does not necessarily convey the opposite message to the discreet one favoured by hotels like the Costes. Take the Schrager hotels as an example, or even the showy style of entrance favoured by the Malmaison in Glasgow. In these cases the entrance is a proud statement that an innovative and interesting design is to be found inside; it is almost the equivalent of the designer label in the world of fashion. The huge doors on Sunset Boulevard that signal the entrance of the Mondrian in Los Angeles (see p. 53) are an unequivocal promise that the rest of the Philippe Starck interior will measure up to the theatricality of the entrance. It is almost a challenge – a device that successfully draws the maximum of attention to the hotel through deliberate overstatement. Inside, the low-ceilinged lobby contrasts with the entrance in a witty play on scale, linking the interior and exterior designs.

Opposite A golden-yellow wall and blue velvet upholstery in the lobby of the Delano, Miami, remind guests of the sand and sea just outside the entrance. But the airy, spacious atmosphere offers a stylish oasis of calm after the hustle and bustle of vibrant beach life.

Similar aims are apparent in the design of the entrance at St Martins Lane (see p. 55), Ian Schrager's first hotel venture in London. The towering revolving door is dramatically lit from above and flanked by glass partitions that are mysteriously shrouded by curtains. So the interior is concealed to a large extent but the occasional glimpse of the lobby is dramatic enough to assure passers-by that this is no ordinary establishment (particularly at night, when the extravagant

'A more open, less stylized design might foster an accessible image that implies people are welcome to come in for a closer look, but the chic, expensive-looking entrance can convey the definite impression that this is a strictly private hotel.'

lighting takes full effect). But the exterior message in this case is twofold. In part the teasing, mysterious façade acts almost as a design preview, like a trailer for the St Martins Lane experience. More significantly, however, the entrance has been designed to intimidate those who do not necessarily know where they are going or exactly what kind of establishment this is (there is no sign to indicate it and the door staff hardly seem approachable). This is evidently a destination for culturally savvy, sophisticated customers who are confident they belong; as for the rest, the entrance is giving them no clues, much less any invitation to come in.

Let there be light

Other aspects of the exterior message, such as lighting, can also have a specific effect on the impact of the entrance doors. One Aldwych in London (see p. 54) is an example of a new hotel with an entrance that delivers a strong message. The classic stone materials that have survived since its days as a banking hall encase the modern glass-and-steel door, communicating that this is a contemporary design hotel, where the emphasis is as much on style as comfort. But the creative use of lighting gives the entrance an entirely different character after nightfall.

Comparing the day and night personalities of the One Aldwych entrance reveals a lot about the ways in which the new hotel can alter its image and consequently manipulate its audience. This effect is achieved in exactly the same way as a good theatre producer might use stage lighting to change the mood or tone of certain scenes.

The daytime look is that of a grand, elegant, yet slightly forbidding establishment – the kind of place where serious business can be conducted in a stylish and sober environment. The night-time look, however, is a completely different story. The entrance is strongly lit from below, just like a painting or sculpture at an exhibition, with the aim of heightening the sense of scale and importance attached to the hotel but also imbuing it with a strong sense of occasion. The drama and theatricality of the lighting radically alter the exterior message of the hotel by changing the character of the entrance to that of a glamorous evening destination.

Image is everything

The staff who man the entrance of a hotel are also an important element of the overall message. The smart grey uniform of the doorman at the Time in New York, for instance, acts as an effective contrast against the backdrop of a fashionable, very modern hotel by suggesting old-fashioned values of service. Conversely, the casually attired doormen at St Martins Lane in London convey the impression that, although this is a sophisticated and expensive hotel, the protocol of jacket and tie does not apply. This in turn directs a subtle message at its audience: the uniform of the staff is designed to attract custom through a kind of inverted snobbery. The casual attire is an indirect form of flattery, intimating that the clientele are likely to be a creative, imaginative crowd who similarly do not need to bother with conventional sartorial formalities.

The lobby

When considered from design and architectural points of view the lobby is perhaps more complex than any other part of the hotel because it is a democratic space. Unlike other areas of

the hotel, the lobby is not private; it has to accommodate a constant flow of residents and non-residents, while at the same time allowing the hotel personnel to perform necessary duties and customer services efficiently but discreetly. It is the epicentre of the hotel and therefore the hub of operations for the manifold duties of the hotel staff. Many new hotels have adopted a novel approach to incorporating these necessary elements of the day-to-day management of the hotel into the design of the lobby.

Spatial significance

As a democratic space, the lobby is forced to assume a variety of different identities at once in order to function both as an independent space in its own right and as a component of the hotel as a whole. It is therefore vital that the designer is able to achieve the kind of balance that allows the lobby to operate as the primary circulation point in a hotel without any risk of it becoming a bottleneck for human traffic. In order to do this the practical and ergonomic considerations of customer flow and checking in and out must be weighed against the equally important need to create a certain style and a strong visual impact that will give the character of the hotel its stamp.

Designers of the new hotel have dealt with these issues in a number of ways, but in order to understand fully the significance of the new approach to lobby design a wider perspective must first be provided. Historically hotel lobbies, such as those at the Ritz in London or Paris, often aimed at a neoclassical reproduction of the entrance to a stately home or famous building. Then came a more modern American approach during the 1970s that introduced a fad for building almost cathedral-like glass atria with a soaring central apse, in an effort to give a more dramatic role to the lobby. The 1980s saw a second, updated trend towards the neoclassical style and during the 1990s the search for ways of creating a theatrical, high-impact lobby continued. At this point the blueprint for the new hotel lobby began to emerge in the work of Philippe Starck, Andrée Putman and Anouska Hempel. The Hempel became in London, for instance, a significant landmark in lobby design, as it brought minimalism, the use of light and Cubist principals into the foreground, thereby subverting many of the accepted principles of lobby design.

'Designers of the new hotel tend to use the lobby as a kind of manifesto for their design intentions in a particular project; it becomes a shorthand statement of the hotel's style.'

Design signature

Designers of the new hotel tend to use the lobby as a kind of manifesto for their design intentions in a particular project; it becomes a shorthand statement of the hotel's style. It is increasingly seen to be the signature of the new hotel, not just of its interior but also of its image as a whole. It is most commonly the lobby that is pictured in publicity material, for example, or that features prominently in high-profile receptions and social events. The task, then, for the designer of the new hotel lobby is to be innovative and imaginative, and, above all, to be able to juggle the issues of budget, functionality, space and volume in order to create the maximum impact.

Inevitably, though, styles change and the customers of the new hotel are no longer looking for volume when they walk into a hotel lobby. Hotels like the Marriott Marquis in New York, with their enormous lobby areas and surrounding balconies leading to the rooms, have now slipped out of fashion, to be replaced by the more restrained concept of lobby design evident in new hotels like the St David's hotel and spa in Cardiff. St David's exemplifies the change in architectural styles: the entrance to the lobby, although clearly not on the same scale as the old style of atrium lobby, still allows the customer to view the rest of the hotel and to get an impression of space and volume. The St David's lobby gives an understanding of the architectural volume and size of the hotel, while preserving a sense of intimacy, privacy and identity at the same time.

The Martinspark in Dornbirn, Austria, achieves a similar balance. The light, natural colour scheme of earthy browns and white offsets the spare design of the lobby, while the raised ceiling and the first-floor balcony give an immediate sense of space. Equally, La Prouse in Nantes introduces wooden floors and surfaces, as well as an abundance of natural light, into an otherwise completely minimal lobby design, thus balancing a strong design statement with an innately warm, almost cosy, feel to the interior.

Let the architecture speak

The inherent architectural features of a building can also supply the designer with the raw materials for creating drama and a strong first impression of the interior. As previously discussed, it is the exterior message of the hotel that generally gives the very first indication of its style, but the information contained in the lobby is the next, more detailed message that elaborates on that first impression.

The towering pillars in the lobby of the SoHo Grand in New York are a fine example of innate architectural features being used to good effect. Contemporary soft furnishings and the very restrained palette of colours used throughout the rest of the lobby counterbalance the sense of grandeur implied by the sheer size of the pillars. By the same token, the natural attributes of the Delano in Miami (see p. 56), although less dramatic than those of the SoHo Grand, are also deftly incorporated into the design. The impact of the Delano's lobby relies largely on the subtle ways in which the building's light and breezy interior has been enhanced. The fabrics that upholster the furniture and the colours on the walls and floor have been chosen to complement the powerful natural light

and the climate of Florida. The result is a warm, stylish and fundamentally theatrical lobby where the furniture and fittings are larger than life.

Dramatic entrances

Ian Schrager's collaborations with various big-name designers have yielded some of the most influential lobbies of the 1990s. Andrée Putman's stylish monochromatic design for the Morgans lobby or Philippe Starck's groundbreaking lobby at the Royalton, where guests feel they are stepping on a fashion catwalk, have both left their mark and sparked numerous imitations. But the lobby at St Martins Lane in London must surely be his most striking achievement yet.

The flourishes of a dramatic design signature are certainly evident in the ornate Louis XVI armchairs and footstools, enormous projections of fish on the doors of the Light Bar, fat pillars and quirky sculptures. The use of spotlighting set into the floor adds a theatrical twist to the colour scheme. But there is also a striking element of surreal humour. Instead of conventional coffee tables, ridiculously kitsch garden gnomes balancing trays on their heads are placed cheekily beside the sumptuously upholstered benches and stools. Giant chess pieces and gold molar-shaped stools bring a kind of Alice in Wonderland fantasy element to the design, which is a type of theatricality in itself but one that also fuels the imagination as well as the desire for glamour and catwalk sophistication.

Above *The lobby at the Royalton, New York, is tailormade for those who like to make an entrance. Conceived by Philippe Starck, it resembles a catwalk along which supermodels and stilettoed socialites may sashay. A welcome for the well-heeled.*

Below left *The ceiling of the lobby at the Belaggio, Las Vegas, is over the top in every sense. A mind-blowing meadow of blown-glass flowers by Dale Chihuly prepares guests to expect the extraordinary – whatever the expense.*

Elaborate design of a slightly different kind is seen in the extraordinary blown-glass ceiling of the lobby at the Bellagio in Las Vegas. The hotel itself is a testament to over-the-top design, with an art collection that could seriously rival the Impressionist vaults of any major European gallery. There is also a unique water feature outside the hotel that has to be seen to be believed (more than 1,000 fountains in front of the hotel are choreographed to musical excerpts spanning classical music, opera and hits from Broadway musicals). Bellagio truly reflects the fact that the lobby of the new hotel often tends to be its design signature. Seeking a trump card that would somehow encapsulate the extravagance of an establishment that also has its own botanical gardens and Mediterranean villa complex, artist Dale Chihuly came up with the Fiori di Como. Covering more than 185 square metres (2,000 square feet) and consisting of more than 2,000 individual pieces of blown glass, the Fiori took two years to complete. The result is a lobby with a ceiling entirely composed of coloured-glass flowers, blooming above dumbstruck customers as they check in to the hotel.

In this case the purpose of the lobby design is to baptize the guest in the hotel's cult of overstatement and opulence – the classic American credo of bigger is better. The lobby at St Martins Lane is clearly light years away from the glass-encrusted spectacle of Bellagio but the two are nevertheless intimately connected. Each, in its own way, serves as a design device enabling the operators of the hotels to lay their cards on the table. It is an opportunity to say to potential customers: this is the kind of experience that awaits you here and this is what you can expect if you choose to stay here.

The design of the lobby can also draw attention to the hotel's immediate surroundings and heighten the visitor's

sense of place as a result. The lobby at the Pier One Parkroyal in Sydney (see p. 64) has a glass floor that is ideally suited to its location, jutting out over the waters of Sydney harbour. The view of the sea beneath the floor is impressive in itself and works well as a design feature but it also ensures that guests are able to appreciate and are reminded of their waterside location even when inside the hotel.

Chill and mix

One of the most important functions of the hotel lobby is to provide a common area in which guests may relax and meet and greet visitors. It is a common concern of many new hotels that the design of the lobby should therefore reflect the nature of the hotel and consequently affect the atmosphere of this communal point, placing it somewhere between the opposite poles of a predominately business or pleasure venue. Two examples of diametrically opposed lobby designs might be those of Edinburgh's Bonham and the Kirketon in Sydney.

In the case of the lobby at the Bonham, the environment is that of a smart townhouse hotel, where there is ample opportunity for guests to ensconce themselves in an easy chair and catch up on some facts and figures before a meeting. The voluptuous scarlet curves of the central seat, with an elegant, oversized lampshade poised just above it, are the kind of details that define this as a hip business hotel for the design-conscious traveller, but a business hotel it is nevertheless. The lobby at the Kirketon, however, sends out an entirely different message. Here the furniture, arranged purely for its design impact, does not invite lingering. This is a hotel lobby aimed at trendy young punters who are not looking for a hotel geared to the needs of the business community; they are here because this is a destination design hotel where image reigns supreme.

The bulk of new hotels are positioned somewhere between these two extremes. The Ripa in Rome, for example, makes a clever design statement with its perfectly symmetrical lobby, where the reception desk is framed by identical staircases sweeping up on either side and the matching sets of carmine armchairs are illuminated from above by a stylish pool of light. Nevertheless, the design of the lobby is not so self-conscious as to banish a feeling that this may be the kind of place where guests could feel comfortable simply relaxing or waiting for a visitor. The same applies to the lobby of the Manor in New Delhi, where the sexy curves of the high-backed sofa and matching coffee table make at once an effective design statement and an inviting space in which to linger.

Right *Straight lines in the lobby of the Ripa, Rome, are softened by spherical lights and assorted pouffes on the floor, symbolizing that efficiency rules here – but with a friendly, human touch.*

Below left *Everything in the Bonham, Edinburgh, adds up to give the message that business is far from boring. A shapely lobby seat and show-off lampshade promise fun playing FTSE.*

What's on offer

It is also common for the new hotel lobby to be linked with or often to incorporate a bar or restaurant that has a strong connection to the hotel itself (see p. 66). Increasingly, then, the lobby acts as a transition point not just for guests on their way to their rooms but also for non-residents heading for amenities where they can have a drink or enjoy a meal. The lobby also provides the main access to the hotel's health and spa facilities.

The lobby is not just a thoroughfare for human traffic; it also has to be a transit point for guests' luggage. Owing to the complex nature of the new hotel lobby, this task must be addressed without disrupting the primary functions of the lobby and with a minimal impact on the carefully crafted mood of the space. An efficient system of baggage handling must therefore be devised and incorporated into the lobby design.

Some new hotels have decided to take an innovative and refreshing approach to the necessary and all too often mundane aspects of hotel life. A good example would be the lifts at the Sanderson in London. Even though elevators are obviously necessary, even essential, to the smooth running of any large hotel, their design is commonly overlooked as they are viewed as banal, insignificant cogs in the building's machinery. The Sanderson, however, has seized on the opportunity to make a design statement by covering the interior of the lifts in hologram-style spacescapes, with a blanket of stars winking in the distance (see p. 59). The impression is that of being suspended in the night sky, transforming the experience of travelling from floor to floor into an impressive, tongue-in-cheek stab at Disneyland space travel. Since every guest in the hotel is almost guaranteed to use the lifts at some point, this design feature is a clever piece of opportunism, impressing on a captive audience the total design commitment of the hotel.

Checking in

It is important to distinguish between the functions of the reception and those of the concierge. The reception and check-in desk is where paperwork is processed, keys are issued to guests and quibbles with bills, surcharges and related matters are dealt with. The concierge, however, tends to fit more into the

category of guest relations, acting as adviser, problem-solver and PA to guests, offering guidance on local affairs and problems with staff or other guests, as well as attending to more mundane duties such as booking tickets and arranging transfers.

Naturally, though, the inevitable starting point of any hotel experience is the process of checking in. Not only is it the first real contact between a customer and the staff of the hotel, it is also the earliest indication of how competently a hotel runs the business end of its operation. The new hotel deals with this crucial process in a variety of ways. First impressions are important and the fundamental purpose of the design of the reception and check-in area is to convey the right balance of friendliness with the key notes of formality and efficiency.

The Time in New York manages to achieve this fine balance. The large illuminated keyhole mounted on the wall behind the reception desk identifies the check-in area in no uncertain terms but it does so with inimitable style and elegance. The openness and humour of the design have a reassuring effect on the customers, and any apprehension is instantly dissolved. More ambitious still is the extraordinary design of the reception area at the Standard in Los Angeles. Immediately behind the desk is a showcase bubble bed where guests can chill out and watch a mini TV suspended from the ceiling, resulting in an

effect that is both highly original and restful. In addition, the front of the desk is lined with Barbarella-style barstools that invite guests to just hop on and enjoy a more laid-back, informal approach to the often rather starchy process of checking in.

A warm reception

Like the rest of the lobby area, the reception of the new hotel is also used as a design signature for the establishment as a whole. The bare, monolithic slab that constitutes the check-in desk at London's Hempel hotel is a succinct expression of the credo of spartan, minimal design that guests can expect to encounter elsewhere in the hotel. Similarly, Christian Liagre's triptych of oversized lampshades that hover above the reception desk at the Mercer in New York (see p. 76) introduce a theme of innovative lighting that is then repeated in the remaining rooms, corridors and lounges.

The Nash in South Beach, Miami, presents a smooth, voluptuous take on reception design. The circular bank of pigeonholes mounted on the wall behind the check-in desk is a pleasing match for the horseshoe shape of the desk itself and the plunging curves of the surrounding alcove. In all it is a simple, solid space that is a refreshingly modern departure from the usual art-deco trappings of South Beach hotels.

The race to create innovative and exciting new slants on how customers check in to a hotel has meant that the reception has rapidly evolved from being a purely organic aspect of hotel life to a prominent part of the portfolio of services and facilities. The advent of the sky lobby, for example, revolutionized the way customers are able to check in to hotels by cutting the main lobby out of the equation completely and substituting a hybrid of business centre and conventional reception.

Concierge calling

The role of the concierge, in contrast to that of reception, has changed quite significantly with the advent of the new hotel and has become a more omnibus post in hotel life. The traditional location of the concierge behind a counter, for example, is perceived to form a barrier to effective customer relations, and in the case of contemporary hotels the concierge is often relocated to a more accessible desk and assigned a role of guest relations. The concierge must be equipped to address the practical requirements of the customer, whether those needs are related to the running of the hotel or not. It is therefore imperative that the physical position of the concierge within the hotel lobby itself reflects this emphasis on openness and approachability.

This line of thinking was very much pioneered by Ian Schrager and is particularly evident in some of his more recent hotels. The Sanderson and St Martins Lane in London both have a concierge desk in the lobby, for example.

Lobby shopping

Another conspicuous feature of the new hotel lobby is a shop selling gifts, books and even furniture that is connected to the design or the designer of the hotel in question. The hotel shop has become a useful barometer of just how much the tastes of the general public are influenced by design hotels. A good indicator might be that guests at St Martins Lane in London are able to buy Philippe Starck wares until three o'clock in the morning, or that the lobby at the Great Eastern Hotel in London stocks the flowers by Wild at Heart that also appear in the hotel's guestrooms.

The ultimate sales pitch of the new hotel is when the actual furnishings (or at least replicas of them) are available for purchase. The Blakes hotels are best known for this approach, which allows customers to buy into the aspirational design of the hotel. In a sense this is the zenith of lifestyle marketing among new hotels; not only is the accommodation itself on offer but there is also the opportunity to buy into the design statement of the hotel on a permanent basis by incorporating it into the private home or office space.

Left *Both guests and non-residents make a beeline for mybar at myhotel, London, lured by the tempting array of alcoholic nectars purposely visible from the adjoining lobby.*

Opposite *The reception desk in the Standard, Los Angeles, invites you to make an exhibition of yourself. Its target clientele are clearly the extrovert and the laid-back.*

elements of style

4

the vocabulary of design

'In order to make a strong design statement the new hotel designer must be aware of the language of contemporary design, its etymology and the flexibility and scope that this vocabulary of styles can offer.'

It is often the case that when a design has to be described in words, the purpose of the design itself has failed. Design is, after all, a visual language and the designer has to choose his vocabulary carefully to make this language clear and to communicate the message. The vocabulary of design is the usual shorthand that transmits the designer's intentions. The choice of an architectural style – whether it be gothic, Renaissance, colonial or Bauhaus – will send the first message. In addition to this, the elements within a room – which will include materials, wallcoverings, curtains, plants and accessories, are all a crucial part of the make up of the overall style. The uses of flowers, types of furniture and textures play an important part in the elements of style.

Every aspect of style must achieve a balance between luxury and vulgarity, opulence and waste, restraint and severity. It is essential, therefore, to create an architecture that encompasses materials relevant to the original brief, and the message and style of the hotel that is being brought to life. For example, a designer might choose a Belgian marble for the classic grand hotel, or a honed limestone for the more contemporary pared-down look.

Creating the vision

Increasingly with the new hotel, the initial stages of a project entail an intensive period of collaboration between the designer and the hotel operator, and this relationship tends to remain very close throughout the entire design process. Their fundamental objective is to establish a clear definition of the hotel's target audience, its intended niche in the market and the nature of its brand. The designer must work with the client specifically to define the remit of that brand and to arrive at an exact understanding of the ways in which the design can be adapted to fit it.

The concept of style as a means of pigeon-holing the aspirations of the general public is therefore pivotal to the success of the new hotel. In this context a designer is not just the interpreter but also the arbiter of taste, making it necessary for many other factors to be taken into account before the practical considerations of the design can be addressed. Most importantly the designer must have an acute awareness of the trends and social changes that affect the lifestyle aspirations of the new hotel's target audience.

One definition of lifestyle is the way in which any given individual chooses to live and how the net result of those choices can be used to define that person. From the cars people drive and the TV programmes they watch, to the way they decorate their homes, the clothes they wear, the restaurants they eat in and their chosen holiday destination, these are the things that define lifestyle. By cultivating a familiarity with the possible outcomes of these choices, the designer is able to lock on to the aspirations of various lifestyle or socio-economic groups and deliver a product that is going

Above *Earthy terracottas and browns warm the white walls of the lounge in the Mercer, New York, and at the same time allude to the building's red-brick exterior.*

to meet their requirements and expectations. The new hotel tends to target a sophisticated, independent consumer whose expectations are high, so all the elements of its design must be chosen with this in mind.

These elements of style are the designer's only tools. Unlike the hotel operator, who imposes a certain style on the hotel in an abstract way (through the management of service, image and protocol), the designer must work strictly within the physical constraints of architecture, such as space allocation, interior furnishings and finishes. In order to make a strong design statement the new hotel designer must be aware of the language of contemporary design, its etymology and the flexibility and scope that this vocabulary of styles can offer.

Colour

In the language of style, colour is one of the richer dialects, ranging from what are essentially subliminal influences through to bold statements of design and identity. At its most remarkable, the use of colour can be a dramatic, even

dominant, feature of the overall design and there are many examples of new hotels that flaunt certain aspects of their design through a marked use of colour. The lounge at the Mercer in New York is certainly one, with the rich reds and browns of its furnishings warmly suffusing the white background of the walls and tall windows. But a more blatant instance of how colour can be used to define the tone and mood of a space would be the Red Suite at the Sofitel St-Jacques in Paris. Various shades of red, spanning deep burgundy to creamy pink, run through the carpets, upholstery, wallpaper and furnishings. Deliberately simple and understated furniture, such as the low, wide bed and plain red bedside units, help to keep the attention focused squarely on the interaction of the different elements of the colour scheme. The result is that this symphony in red produces an image of decadence and lipstick glamour that owes everything to the fact that the rich, sensual colours are allowed to dominate and ultimately define the character of the room.

The Time in New York takes this principle a step further by using colour to divide its accommodation into three distinct categories: red, yellow and blue rooms. Aside from this variation in colour, there are no ostensible differences between the three types of room, so the function of colour as a catalyst for changing the character and feel of a physical space is emphasized to the greatest possible extent. When checking in to the hotel, guests can base their choice of room purely on which colour happens to suit their mood at the time, without having to worry about which room has better amenities or a more appealing design.

Opulence

The theatrical potential of colour is commonly exploited by designers of the new hotel, who have taken their cue from seminal interiors like the heavy, chintzy opulence of the Hôtel Costes in Paris or the black-lacquered woods and dark, dusky complexion of Blakes in London. Indeed Blakes in Amsterdam (see pp. 158–63) also relies heavily on specific colours to create a context for the design as a whole: one of the bedrooms, for instance, draws its inspiration from the Dutch East India Company with paints and fabrics ranging from ginger to turmeric. This provides an apt and unmistakably contemporary setting for the antique furniture that lies dotted around the room. Elsewhere, traditional Dutch shades of green, navy and black are intended to recall the inky tones of a Rembrandt, while biscuity patches of exposed brick chase away the shadows.

Restraint

James Soane of Conran & Partners favoured a similarly correct colour scheme when working on the Great Eastern Hotel in London. Original plasterwork and mouldings have been meticulously preserved in many of the public areas, and the majority of the colours throughout the hotel were chosen from the historically accurate National Trust range. The overall effect is to transpose the classic British demeanour of restraint and quiet confidence into the fabric of the design. Often the colours are sober, even muted, but they seem all the more potent for it, highlighting the original features of the building and creating a cool, soothing environment for guests.

Colour can also be a powerful form of understatement, of which perhaps the most influential example has been the white-on-white effect created by Philippe Starck at the Delano in Miami (see p. 75). The discreet, Armani-inspired neutral tones of the Four Seasons hotels or the coloured lighting in the lobby of St Martins Lane in London are other gentle reminders of how less can in fact mean more in design terms.

Left *Colours are primary in the bedrooms of the Time, New York: alike in every other respect, they differ only in being either all red, all blue or all yellow. Blue bestows calm and tranquillity, red resonates with passion and drama.*

Above right *At the Hôtel Costes, Paris, designer Jacques Garcia expressed his exuberant love of excess. Furniture, wallpapers, rugs, fabrics and lamps were all specially made to recapture the richesse of France's Second Empire.*

The bedrooms at the Seehof in Zurich also manage to capture an air of slick modernity through the restrained use of colour. Almost everything is white: walls, bedlinen, furniture, fabrics and fittings, even the flowers, contribute to the whitewash effect. Here the designer set the stage for a few subtle streaks of colour, such as the lemon fabric used for the curtains or the brushed silver of the table.

Texture

By choosing materials that have a highly distinctive texture, the designer can enhance and manipulate the various effects of colours and finishes. The indulgent nature of the new hotel dictates that its design should aim to stimulate the senses at all times, and incorporating unusual or contrasting textures, even in the subtlest forms, is an effective way of doing just that.

The fine work of Christian Liagre at the Montalambert in Paris shows an acute awareness of how contrasting textures can be used to maximize the impact of certain materials. This is particularly evident in the lobby, where patinated bronze picture frames and jagged metalwork are juxtaposed against the perfectly smooth surface of the limestone floor. The result is pleasing to the eye, as it accentuates the qualities of the materials: the hard, solid slabs of limestone are more striking in their bare simplicity next to the rough and deliberately imperfect finish of the bronze.

It is not only materials and finishes that are linked to texture: colour also has its place in the equation. By varying the texture of fabrics and materials, the effects of colour can be greatly enhanced. This is particularly noticeable in furniture upholstery, as with the bedroom armchairs at the TriBeCa Grand in New York (see p. 74). The copper of the armchair beside the bed is a welcome disruption of the smooth purple and blue tones of the rest of the room, and the effect of this contrast is undeniably heightened by the panne texture of the upholstery.

The nap of the fabric gives a tactile sheen to the burnished colour of the armchair, which both points up the sober palette of background colours and provides some necessary drama to the eye.

The library installation in the Bel Etage restaurant at the Teufelhof in Basel is a singular example of the use of texture in new hotel design. The installation consists of rows of old books that have been roughly cemented into a frame, with the uneven layers of white cement left oozing out between them. The effect is rather like that of lashings of cream or icing on a cake. The work thus has a sensuous, evocative texture that stimulates the senses and is hence appropriate to its culinary setting. The use of texture in this case is not merely evocative but also contextual, as the designer uses a ruse reminiscent of food to remind customers subtly where they are and why they are there.

Finishes

Clear, simple finishes are synonymous with the current trend for minimalist design among new hotels but their appeal must be weighed against the necessity for fabrics and finishes that are equal to the wear and tear of hotel life. The designer needs to find the right compromise between style and durability in

order to create an interior that will stand the test of time. Overlooking these practical considerations can result in a premature need for refurbishment due to the rapid disintegration of materials that have become worn and shabby because they are simply too delicate for the job.

Interior lighting

Unlike the other elements of style already discussed in this chapter, interior lighting can be constantly updated and adjusted with very little, if any, disruption to the running of the hotel. Lighting should be looked upon as the life force of any successful interior and is therefore the one particular aspect of the overall style that should be versatile.

Above *Philippe Starck's influential bedroom interiors at the Delano, Miami, have a conventual purity: linens, walls, ceilings, floors and furniture are virginally white. Yet the genius of the design means that the effect is neither cold nor clinical, but one of calm contemplation.*
Above left *White-on-white bedrooms in the Mercer, New York, express a similarly pared-down style accentuating the sense of space and light associated with loft-living. Simplicity does not imply skimping, though – the sheets are Frette, the furniture custom made.*
Opposite *In a bedroom at the TriBeCa Grand, New York, muted colours allow texture to become the focus of attention. Low-key lighting plays over rough-weave linens on the bed, smooth walls, a simple, ridged vase and a shimmering velvet armchair. All are temptingly tactile, imparting a restrained and sophisticated sense of luxury.*

Left *Christian Liagre lights above the reception desk in the Mercer, New York, are generously sized to match the hotel's warehouse dimensions, yet greet guests with a warm, welcoming glow.*

Right *Natural and artificial light are cleverly choreographed in the bedrooms of The Hôtel, Lucerne, to create sensual interiors that mirror the evocative film stills projected onto the ceilings.*

Below *As if in a gallery, precisely positioned spotlights illuminate an Arne Jacobsen chair in a corridor of the Prince, Melbourne. Wicker lampshades supply a textural contrast.*

A hotel is a 24-hour business and the onus is on the designer to ensure that the effect of the chosen lighting is unobtrusive at all times of day and night. Just as importantly, however, the interior lighting of a hotel must also be strong enough to exert a palpable influence on the surroundings and to create different moods at different times of day. As with the rest of new hotel design, then, the secret to successful lighting lies in harmony and balance.

However, lighting has become more than just a design consideration. The new hotel has ushered in an era of consumerism that places more emphasis than ever on isolating the specific details that make an interior unique. Marketing and the media continue to elevate the more innovative designers to a status of virtual superstardom, and then it is only a matter of time before high-street department stores are stocking mass-market imitations of their work. Lighting in particular seems to attract more attention than almost anything else, so

choosing the light fixtures in a contemporary hotel has become an opportunity for designers to make their mark.

Some seminal developments include Christian Liagre's double-diffused parchment lights at the Mercer in New York, which were an early example of how lighting can be deployed to give a warming, even humanizing, effect to a spare, contemporary interior. Equally, Andrée Putman's lighting at the Morgans and Philippe Starck's rhinoceros lights at the Royalton, both in New York, sparked fresh trends. At the start of the twenty-first century, though, the use of lighting in the new hotel has clearly evolved beyond the influence of these pioneering examples.

A particularly original approach is the light sculpture that was created for the Teufelhof in Basel: here a bedside lamp projects a refracted beam of light on to the opposite wall, depicting shards of broken glass. The installation is even accompanied by sounds of shattered glass tinkling to the floor.

This is an example of innovative lighting at its most far-fetched but it is also important to note how the effect of such a feature, although significant, does not have to be permanent. In other words, it is an animate component of the design that can be turned on and off at the flick of a switch, thereby giving the customer a greater degree of control than normal over the mood and ambience of the surroundings.

'Lighting should be looked upon as the life force of any successful interior and is therefore the one aspect of the overall style that should be versatile.'

The discreet ceiling lighting at The Hôtel in Lucerne (see p. 77), Switzerland, is also a highly effective device, as it works in harmony with a particularly innovative series of art installations. French architect Jean Nouvel has devised an interior that uses giant still photographs to decorate the ceilings of the guestrooms. A blow-up of selected film scenes covers each of the ceilings in all 25 suites and studios at The Hôtel. Discreet localized lighting enhances the impact of these ceiling pictures and, when seen from outside – particularly at night – it produces the spectacle of a glowing patchwork of colour (see p. 50).

Lighting the mood

Creating the right mood for the occasion is clearly the primary function of lighting in an environment such as the new hotel, where every space has its distinct identity. The TriBeCa Grand in New York, for instance, creates a tranquil enclave, away from the brick and iron girders of its predominantly industrial design, with a specially designed candlelight fireplace. Around 80 paraffin candles are encased behind myriad small coloured-glass lenses in a multicoloured homage to the primal home comforts of a fire. The contrast between the warmth of the candlelight and the sturdy manmade aesthetics of the warehouse setting adds an intelligent, witty dimension to the design.

Philippe Starck's lighting of the Delano in Miami is similarly astute. Natural light, which is maximized during the day by the open design of the lobby, is replaced at night by the intimate and romantic combination of new and vintage lights, carefully arranged candles and nightlights. The contrast is, once again, extreme and serves to illustrate how the careful use of lighting can dramatically transform the mood and tone of a space.

The design of the XV Beacon in Boston is aiming for an image of a modern, sassy hotel with quiet overtones of townhouse traditionalism, and the apt choice of lighting contributes to this end. The light at the bottom of the ornate, gilded banister of the staircase, for instance, resembles the kind of archaic streetlamp that is immediately associated with Dickens's smog-shrouded London. Directly behind the lamp is a large canvas of modern art, in black and grey tones that would seem to call for strong lighting, but instead of opting for a contemporary form of lighting to suit the nature of the picture, the designer chose to make a statement. The contrast between the historic, grandiose mien of the archaic lamp and the resolute modernity of the picture not only encapsulates the character of the hotel as a whole but also works on the level of imaginative, memorable lighting that defies the accepted notion of matching like with like.

Lighting the design message

The new hotel tends to offer something more than the standard ceiling spotlights, diffused panel lighting and other essentially innocuous light fittings by focusing on what the aesthetic value of a light fitting can contribute to the design message of the hotel. The reception of the Great Eastern Hotel in London (see p.16) is a prime model of this approach. Concealed spotlights are studded around the ceiling but they provide only the background lighting, whereas centre stage is monopolized by the three chrome standard lamps that are fixed to the marble top of the counter. Set in a smart and orderly row, they represent everything that an efficient hotel reception should be but their plain, cylindrical shades also mirror the clean, circular lines of the lobby rotunda above. Here, then, the choice of lighting is not just a question of how to highlight the check-in area; the underlying objective is to create a design that complements the surrounding architecture and expresses the overall design intentions of the hotel.

The overhanging lampshades in the lounge at the Standard in Los Angeles also say something about the hotel's design intentions. On one level the chrome-bubble design brings to mind a typical 1970s film set, which fits in perfectly with the carpeted walls and other kitsch furnishings, but the shape of

Opposite Castiglioni Arco lamps bend elegantly over the lounge at the Standard, Los Angeles. In homage to these 1962 design classics, the pouffes on the shagpile carpet echo their spherical contours.

the lights is also an important consideration. The spherical contours of the lampshades are an exact match with the round, moulded stools and armchairs that are scattered about the rest of the room. It is not enough for the tone of the light fittings to match the image of the hotel; in order to become a powerful design statement they must also blend effectively on a physical level with the aesthetics and configuration of their immediate surroundings.

Furniture

Unlike colour, texture or lighting, a piece of furniture is not so much a subliminal element of style but a self-contained, stand-alone work of art in itself. The size and positioning of furniture in a hotel can often mean that it is one of the first aspects of the design to be noticed. It is also a practical element of the design and, as such, can be appreciated on a number of levels – it must look good but it must also be well made, comfortable and durable. The choice of furniture is therefore a key opportunity for the designer to stamp a particular style and identity on the surroundings in a very clear and immediate way.

The kind of furnishings found in the new hotel varies enormously, perhaps more so than any other element of the design, encompassing cutting-edge, contemporary styles and designs with historic or ethnic influences. Furniture has an intrinsic value and an artistic integrity all of its own; it is more than a mere component of a hotel's design and is therefore more likely to be unusual or unique in appearance. Designing a piece of furniture permits greater freedom of expression than other features and offers a more versatile canvas with fewer restrictions on form and location. Restrictions do still exist, of course, and a disciplined furniture design will recognize the practical issues of functionality along with those of aesthetics and innovation. But the fact remains that if the new hotel is the crucible of modern style then furniture is an indispensable part of its design statement.

The tall, curved design of the conversation corner at the Mondrian in Los Angeles is one of the most well-known examples of contemporary hotel furniture. Its expanse of buttoned crimson upholstery and the sweeping backrest lend a conspiratorial air to this corner of the lobby, and its location, size, colour and flamboyant design mean that it cannot possibly go unnoticed. It is one of this glamorous hotel's strongest design statements.

Marc Newson's wooden chairs in the lobby of the Hempel in London constitute another seminal example. The minimalist background of this lobby is like a blank canvas, enabling the designer to achieve considerable impact without resorting to the elaborate tactics employed by Philippe Starck at the Mondrian. Instead the simplicity of Newson's design speaks volumes, as the rich colour of the wood and buxom curve of the seat are accentuated to the full by the contrasting angular white surroundings.

The high-backed armchair next to the reception at the Malmaison in Manchester is a compromise between these two extremes of understatement and overstatement. It blends in well with the dark fixtures and the exposed brick of the lobby area but it also catches the eye thanks to its disproportionate size. The vertical stripes exaggerate the effect of the high back, yet its position next to a side table and the warm colours of the upholstery invite the assumption that this is also a chair designed for sitting in and not just for its aesthetic contribution.

In the case of contemporary hotels that are more easily defined as lifestyle rather than design hotels, like the Beach

Above *From the ridiculous to the sublime: Philippe Starck has elevated the garden gnome from object of derision to object of desire with these quirky occasional tables in the lobby of the St Martins Lane, London.*

Left *Against the barest of backdrops, Marc Newson's wooden chairs take centre stage in the lobby of the Hempel, London. Nothing distracts the eye from appreciating the intricate design and incredible craftsmanship.*

House at Hermosa Beach in Los Angeles, furniture often places a greater emphasis on comfort than on image or appearance. This hotel is intended as a hip crash-out for party-weary kids and escapists heading for the beach and, as such, it has deep, squashy sofas designed with just one thing in mind: providing something to sink in to and relax in.

At the opposite end of the spectrum, the multicoloured painted chair in the Teufelhof in Basel conveys an entirely different message. This is a hotel with two theatres; it is a place where people come to be intellectually stimulated and pursue cultural activities and the design of the furniture reflects this. The hard wooden form of the chair is not inviting guests to sit down and relax but merely to appreciate its aesthetic qualities and see it as an interesting alternative to conventional furniture design. The emphasis here is placed squarely on appearance, not on comfort.

Escapism through furniture

Furniture that challenges traditional expectations – like the garden-gnome tables at St Martins Lane in London – can also be a powerful tool for creating a specific mood or image. In the St Martins Lane lobby, the furniture is designed to give the space a surreal and fantastical quality. Stools resembling huge golden teeth (see p. 58) are nothing short of bizarre and curious customers who settle themselves on one are absorbed into an environment that is far removed from what is commonly perceived as normal. In this case, the effect of the furniture design is to create a kind of escapist glamour and to conjure up an atmosphere that thrives on its distance from everyday life. This is a magical place where guests can retreat into a pretend world, spirited away from the stresses and strains of everyday responsibility.

Another method of fostering an escapist quality in an interior is to incorporate a historic or ethnic character into the design of the furniture. This tactic is particularly rife among contemporary hotels since it allows the designer to quell the need for escapism and to meet the aspirations of the modern consumer. In the first instance Ethnic or antique furniture establishes a strong association in the mind of the visitor: the suggestion is of a place or time that is not his or her own, consequently bestowing a degree of separation from the pressures of ordinary life. Secondly, the innate exoticism of ethnic designs also conjures up a fantasy life that helps to distance the visitor from the more mundane aspects of his or her own lifestyle.

The Aman hotels exploit this technique adeptly, as does Blakes in Amsterdam (see pp. 158–163), with its flourishes of colonial Dutch furniture, and the Portobello in London, with its Woosterish touches of traditional England.

Artwork

Artwork has traditionally played an important part in the interior design of hotels; examples range from César Ritz's acquisition of fine artworks for the opening of his hotels in Paris and London through to the collection at the Four Seasons in Lisbon during the 1950s. But the use of art in these contexts was still stiff and formal in comparison to its deployment in the new hotel; it was displayed as if in a gallery and was not always congruous with the surroundings. The contemporary viewpoint has a more evolved sense of the place of art in the design manifesto of the hotel.

One of the primary aims of the Great Eastern Hotel in London, for instance, is to provide the necessary defibrillation to revive the weakening pulse of a great British institution – the grand railway hotel – and bring it back to life. The sense of place is also very strong, this establishment being the first hotel to be opened within the Square Mile of the City of London. As a result, much of the artwork in the hotel has been commissioned from artists in the nearby enclaves of Hoxton and Whitechapel. The dual aim of this selective policy towards the hotel's artwork is, first, to create a strong reminder of location by commissioning local British talent and, in so doing, secondly, to reinforce the quasi-patriotic intentions that lay behind the very conception of the hotel in the first place.

In the endless challenge of embedding a theme in a contemporary hotel, art can also become a useful device for making an image stick. The right choice of material can significantly bolster the theme, as in the case of the Hotel du Vin in Bristol, England, which has a giant modern painting of a bottle of wine hanging over the bedhead in one of its bedrooms. This may lack the subtlety of discreet lighting or carefully chosen textures and colours, but it is nevertheless a design technique that is frequently used to good effect.

This is not, however, the only function of artwork in hotel design. Like furniture, art also has an intrinsic value of its own and the impact of a striking work of art in a conspicuous position should not be underestimated. The galleried bar area that surrounds the lobby at the Martinspark in Dornbirn, Austria, is the supreme example of this. The prominent feature of this otherwise subdued, even rather forgettable, mezzanine is a piece titled Physical Sculpture No 5 Vorstudie Documenta IX. This is a floor-to-ceiling glass screen with a three-dimensional image printed on to it. The misleading perspective makes it hard for the onlooker to tell at first glance what it actually is or how it fits in the space and, in this way, it captivates its audience. So, although it is reticent enough not to overpower the surroundings, this sculpture is still the dominant design feature.

However, the most extraordinary example of the union between art and contemporary hotel design must be the Bellagio resort in Las Vegas. This development of luxury accommodations has ram-raided the world of fine art,

Right and opposite *Furnishings function as installation pieces in the public areas of the Prince, Melbourne. Relieved of decades of decorative detritus, the building revealed its grand dimensions, which proved the perfect environment for a collection of contemporary work by Newson, Eames, Botta and young local designers. The honeyed hues of the original timber floorboards complement those of a modern sculptural chair, clean-cut table or plastic chair, and an abundance of space allows each object due attention in the scheme of things.*

acquiring a $200 million haul of mostly Impressionist paintings on which its guests may feast their eyes. This project elevates – or arguably reduces – the use of artwork in hotel design to near theme-park proportions yet it is not inconsistent with the rest of the hotel. After all, a hotel that has a water feature consisting of more than 1,000 fountains in the middle of the Nevada Desert is hardly going to content itself with a few Van Gogh prints in the guestrooms.

In Florence the Gallery Hotel Art combines a fully functional art gallery with a slick new hotel interior courtesy of the Salvatore Ferragamo fashion group. The hotel shares many of the hallmarks of the contemporary hotel discussed in the preceding chapters but it is unique in its ambition to create what its promotional literature hails as a new genre of art. This translates as a constantly changing art exhibition throughout the ground floor of the hotel. It is an experiment on behalf of

the hotel operators to encourage the public to adopt a new, less formal approach to modern art, so that guests find time in their holiday or business schedules for some serious scrutiny of the pieces on display.

Accessories

Traditionally the public spaces of a hotel – the corridors, staircases and landings – have rarely been the focus of the designer's attentions, but the new hotel is characterized by an innate unwillingness to waste any space that could be used to perpetuate and emphasize individual style or character. Whether it is an incidental vase, sculpture or a striking piece of contemporary furniture that makes a strong statement of its own, or the imaginative use of a building's existing architectural quirks, the fact remains that it is attention to detail that sets the design hotel apart from the rest.

The Townhouse in Miami, for example, repeats its mantra of youthful high spirits with corridors that are scattered with water fountains and bench seats stacked with comic books. As mentioned above, the Hotel Gallery Art in Florence takes a rather more high-brow stance on the matter and prefers to adorn its ground-floor space with a constantly changing exhibition of contemporary art. Though very different, both of these practices make clear the kind of lifestyle and the kind of clientele that the hotel is seeking to nurture.

The Prince in Melbourne has left the majority of its public spaces rather spartan and chosen instead to dress these stages with striking pieces of modern furniture by designers such as Newson, Eames and Botta (see pp. 82–3). Unlike in the Townhouse, these are not chairs that invite the guests to make a pitstop *en route* to their room: they are works of art that demand to be taken seriously and they dominate the space that they occupy.

Sound architecture

It would be stating the obvious to say that designers and architects are confined to working within the three spatial dimensions, and yet the concept of sound architecture – which is becoming increasingly common in the public areas of new hotels – seems to challenge this premise. The idea that the designer can refine his or her control over an interior space by playing music that conforms to the lifestyle aspirations of a hotel and its guests is high on the agenda of many cutting-edge hotel projects.

The soundtrack to hotel life has long been a crucial issue and forward-thinking hotel groups like W Hotels have already created bespoke CDs for their guests. After all, what better way to corner a lifestyle market than to offer the target audience sounds (as well as surroundings) that fit their tastes? The Hôtel Costes in Paris also has its own soundtrack for the twenty-first-century guest; while the Great Eastern Hotel in London and others pride themselves on an extensive library of music for guests to peruse. But the Great Eastern Hotel has taken this a step further and, through its collaboration with London-based music specialists Sound Architecture, has established an extra dimension to its interior design.

Door numbers and door keys

The door to a hotel room can be seen, from a design viewpoint at least, as a miniature of the hotel's entrance – it transmits the exterior message of the room just as the hotel entrance projects the exterior message of the hotel. The seemingly trivial detail of how to

tackle the necessary considerations of door numbering and keys becomes significant when seen in this light. Here is an opportunity to give the style and design of a room impact from the outside. It is also an opportunity for the designer to bring individual character to the long corridors that are the bane of most hotel designs.

The new hotel posits a number of theories on the subject: some favour electronic smart cards as the best form of room security, others are steadfast in their choice of large, chunky keys. The ways in which doors are numbered and rooms identified is also an integral and varied aspect of hotel branding. For example, is giving a room a name necessarily better than the clinical objectivism of a number?

Conran Design Partnership has given the rooms at myhotel in London a snappy identity by posting the room numbers by the side of the door on back-lit Perspex sheets. The eye is led down the corridor by these little beacons of light and the space is elevated above the status of a blank row of rooms, which is the accepted norm for any hotel corridor. Instead the design manages to instil a sense of personality and novelty – the corridor is distinguishable from other hotel corridors of the world and is therefore memorable.

The Mercer in New York prefers to show the room number in parenthesis, as if to suggest that what room you are in is really not important: the service is personalized to you. In a similar vein, the Bleibtreu in Berlin illuminates its room numbers in mini portholes to counter the sterile stamp of a number and the resultant fear that the guests' identity may be swamped by a tide of anonymous corridors and passageways.

The Hôtel Square in Paris is another modern hotel offering a contemporary solution to the problem of how to identify rooms. The room numbers are discreetly woven into the

Above right *As well as being discreetly engraved on the doors of the guestrooms at La Villa, Paris, numbers glow like embers on the floor below.*
Right *Each room at the Pelican, Miami, is decorated and named to a theme, and each door announces its unique attributes shamelessly. A picture-frame surround reinforces the impression of stepping into a fantasy world. The upended 'psychedelic (ate) girl' sign is a foretaste of the zingy, pop art experience beyond.*
Far right *Set unobtrusively low down, the subdued and backlit room numbers at the Pousada Santa Maria de Flor da Rosa, Portugal, are entirely appropriate: the quiet modern aesthetic sustains the serenity of the converted ancient monastery.*

carpeted threshold of the door. Ian Schrager has more adventurously adopted this technique in a number of his hotels but the room numbers at the Square retain an elegant simplicity that still seems fresh and innovative, despite the flattering competition.

Innovations in key technology, such as customer recognition through voice and fingerprint data, will no doubt drive considerations of room numbering into obsolescence in years to come. Already these kinds of systems are manifesting themselves in more technologically advanced hotels, but they are still not a fully established part of the design portfolio.

Christening rooms

Naming rooms can be a way for smaller hotels to avoid the cardinal sin of numbering, stamping and processing its guests like cattle at an auction. A notable example of this approach would be the funky Pelican in Miami (see p. 85), owned by the fashion trailblazer Diesel. The rooms are all individually named and each has its distinctive theme, although these are not always obvious with names like Do the Vehicle, Birth of the Bubbles and With Drill.

The bed

The defining accessory of a hotel is, of course, the bed. Despite the many, more superficial reasons why the modern consumer might be attracted to the new hotel, at the end of the day (quite literally) it is the need for accommodation, more specifically for a bed, that is the primary motivation. Consequently the bed is the one feature above all with which designers are expected to be increasingly imaginative and offer new interpretations and innovations. It is the most intimate channel of communication between the designer and the customer and, as a result, the design of the bed is a powerful means of reminding the visitor of the hotel's commitment to style, comfort and service.

The most important consideration when it comes to bed design should always be comfort. The right materials can make the difference between an adequate product and a luxury experience and, no matter how pleasing the aesthetics, if a bed is uncomfortable it is badly designed. The W Hotel group, for instance, insists that every bed in each of its hotels benefits from pillow-top mattresses, 250-thread-count linens and goose-feather duvets. The Prince in Melbourne spoils guests with mohair rugs on every bed (see p. 98), and the Townhouse in Miami panders to aching backs by providing enormous squishy pillows among which guests may nestle and relax completely.

The XV Beacon in Boston pampers its guests with a modern interpretation of the four-poster bed, as does the Four Seasons in Milan, where a bold, contemporary style of four-poster establishes the bed as the main focus of the room.

The bedhead – a signpost

The design of the bed is clearly very important and is not just a question of appearance. Valuable storage space can often be incorporated into the bed unit, as with the bedheads at the Seehof in Zurich. But theatricality is definitely the strength of the new hotel bedhead; in fact, it has almost become a tradition after the seminal work of Philippe Starck at the Paramount in New York.

The Best Whorehouse room at the Pelican in Miami, for example, has a decadent, quilted bedhead surrounded by red-shaded lamps that oozes Old New Orleans sex appeal. It is often the case that the bedhead becomes the central design focus for the guestroom in the new hotel. The Lindrum in Melbourne subtly extends the bedhead up to the ceiling of its guestrooms by positioning swags of the curtain material directly behind the headboard. The Time in New York opts for a much bolder approach with a distended, almost disproportionate,

Opposite *Say it loud, say it clear: in each bedroom of the Time, New York, a huge headboard, massive mattress and clarion colour make an exclamation mark of a bed.*

Above *It is guests' prerogative to change their minds: an interactive mood-lighting system by Isometrix means that merely by turning a dial every guestroom at St Martins Lane, London, can be changed from white to pink, blue, red or green.*

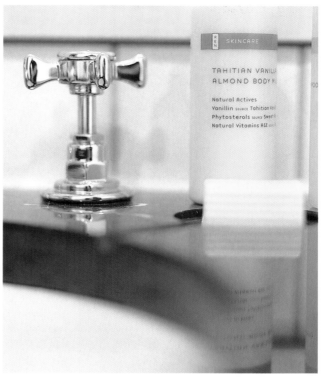

bedhead that acts as the main banner for the room's colour scheme – all the rooms are clad in one of the three primary colours. Similarly, the Manor in New Delhi uses the design of the bedhead to create a motif that is elaborated upon elsewhere in the guestroom. The broad black stripe on the bedhead flows down on to the bedlinen and is also echoed in the design of the carpet and the upholstery of the sofa.

Bathroom bliss

Customers of the new hotel are no longer content with the token towelling wrap hanging on the bathroom door, cheap sheets or bland, uninspiring toiletries. The design commitment must be total, and contemporary hotels are becoming increasingly aware of the need to form strategic alliances with stylish, fashionable boutique lines or large established companies that manufacture toiletries and beauty products. Bed linen, pillows, cushions and bathroom accessories must also reflect the identity of the rest of the hotel, through branding and commitment to quality, and through the elements of style that characterize the rest of the interior, such as colour or texture.

The Prince in Melbourne supplies its guests with Aesop toiletries, and REN toiletries adorn the bathrooms at the Great Eastern Hotel. Bulgari products are provided at the Regent Wall Street, while Aveda is the chosen brand of the W Hotels group

and the TriBeCa Grand has opted for Kiehl's. The Westbourne hotel in London offers its guests a selection of Space NK beauty products. The list goes on. Other new hotels, such as the XV Beacon in Boston or the Time in New York, display a bespoke range of toiletries that bears the hotel's name and logo – the assumption in this case being that no branding opportunity should be wasted.

Above and above left *A guest's every conceivable need is anticipated at the Great Eastern Hotel, London. Bathrooms are charmingly equipped with necessaries, beautifully presented in packaging that matches the colours of the bathroom floor and mat, and features designs inspired by old railway tickets. Toiletries are supplied by REN, a niche company beloved of beauty editors for its chemical-free products.*
Opposite *Bedrooms in the Mercer, New York, are sanctuaries, composed not to stimulate but to soothe the senses. Christian Liagre's faithfulness to white throughout fosters a sense of lightness of being, as do the high ceilings bequeathed by the building's warehouse past.*

room service

5

the hidden experience

'However it is used, the bedroom is still the most private and intimate area of a hotel and, as such, it signifies the destination beyond the destination.'

Contemporary lifestyles and busy executives have rendered the traditional image of the hotel redundant. The idea of a hotel as a destination strictly for tourists has been usurped by one of a more complex package that caters to the varied needs of the modern traveller. The resulting new hotel in some ways defies categorization, since the necessity to be all things to all people is at the very heart of its existence. The design must be flexible enough to provide the right atmosphere for any given occasion, whether its guests require a high-tech office environment or a discreet sanctuary from their busy lives.

Very often this principle of adaptability is more apparent in the bedroom than in any other area of the contemporary hotel. The prevailing reason for this is that the bedroom is still the central focus and the most important part of hotel life, despite the meteoric rise of design and boutique hotels during the final years of the twentieth century. The fires of modern consumerism have forged the more recent phenomena of health clubs, style bars and destination restaurants but the

significance of the hotel bedroom has not been diminished as a result. It can be a simple refuge, a rest point after a long journey or perhaps a romantic location tinged with glamour and excitement. However it is used, the bedroom is still the most private and intimate area of a hotel and, as such, it signifies the destination beyond the destination. It is a microcosm of the design hotel experience that can be enjoyed behind closed doors.

Perhaps because of this need for an all-purpose yet intimate space, the bedroom is often the most gruelling test of a designer's imagination and ingenuity. Accommodating the myriad demands of the twenty-first-century guest in such a confined area is clearly not an easy task and this element of flexibility must not eclipse the practical considerations – the walls, bed, floor and furniture coverings must still be durable and easy to keep clean.

Besides resolving this battle between functionality and design, the contemporary hotel bedroom must establish a degree of consumer autonomy. Guests must have some control over their private environment. One increasingly common example of this is in-room technology, such as email and internet access, that enables customers to create their own schedules and continue their normal routines unimpeded by hotel regimes and restrictions. Essential elements of the design, such as storage space or lighting, need to help guests feel more at home and less like transient visitors. The design machine has swept away Gideon bibles, Corby trouser-

Opposite With high ceilings and areas of exposed concrete, the bedrooms at the Chambers, New York, are reminiscent of a SoHo loft. However, the designer has made sure that the industrial feel of the rooms does not send out the message that corners have been cut. Utilitarian elements are balanced by the care that has been taken to furnish the must-haves of the metropolitan traveller, from scented candles to computer disks.

presses and caustic toiletries, replacing them with new interiors bristling with technology and touched by the wands of luxury, style and fashion.

And so to bed

The bed is not just an essential element of the bedroom but of the hotel as a whole. It has considerable symbolic impact – after all, when stripped down to the bare essentials, what is a hotel if not a place where someone can find a bed for the night? As a piece of furniture the bed is the focal point of the room, both physically and psychologically. It needs to be comfortable, well proportioned and inviting, but most important is the question of where it should be positioned in the room.

Depending on the type and location of the hotel, the bed can be positioned facing, opposite to or parallel with the window. In most cases it is unwise to locate the bed against or adjacent to a window, since this makes potential problems associated with light and climate control much harder to overcome.

The new hotel tends to apply a certain degree of lateral logic to the question of storage space around the bed. It might be an area of box shelving incorporated into the bedhead, an appendage to the side of the bed or a facility utilizing the space beneath the bed. Bedside tables are essential, along with some form of bedside lighting. Irrespective of the quality or ingenuity of the design, there must also be enough room to accommodate an inevitable clutter of books, magazines, drinking glasses and the like. Once again, the dictates of functionality assert themselves and the designer is compelled to work within limited parameters.

It may be a debate that is far from resolved in other aspects of bedroom life but, in terms of the hotel bed at least, size definitely does matter. Large beds are synonymous with comfort and luxury, and their dimensions tend to have a direct bearing on the price and prestige of a room. Most beds are designed to accommodate two people and the designer should always bear in mind the possibility of double occupancy when thinking about how the facilities and technology will be operated. Most people would not expect to have to leave their bed in a hotel to switch off the light, operate the TV or use the telephone but the new hotel is apt to offer an even greater degree of control.

The TriBeCa Grand in New York is an example of a new hotel that caters to a kind of modern lifestyle that does not always draw a distinct line between work and relaxation.

Internet access can be gained via the TV console (see p. 101) and is operated through wireless keyboards that come as standard in all rooms. This enables guests to browse the web or even to work from the comfort of their bed, giving them the maximum possible flexibility to merge the boundaries between their professional and personal lives if they so wish.

The bedroom should be furnished with a view to cosseting the guest and creating an atmosphere of comfort and indulgence. With this in mind, at least one comfortable chair per occupant is an essential addition.

Out of the closet

The allocation of the storage space in a hotel bedroom is a continual balancing act, wherein the necessity to economize with space has to be offset against the need to create as much storage room as possible. It can often be a temptation for hotel

Above *At the Metropolitan, London, bedrooms maintain the hotel's philosophy of refined restraint. Quality, sophisticated simplicity and ease are expressed in custom-made bedheads, blond woods and demure lamps that provide just the right degree of ambient or task lighting.*

Opposite *Every facet of the Hempel, London, seeks to bestow on guests the blessings of Zen serenity. In one room the exquisitely ascetic bed area is suspended on a delicate pine platform that appears to float above the room, raising sleepers to a higher plane of consciousness.*

operators (particularly in conversions or in structures where space is especially limited) to overlook the issue of storage in an attempt to squeeze in a greater number of rooms. This is a false economy that must be avoided at all costs, since the results of stingy allocation of storage space never go unnoticed and it can prove to be the Achilles heel of an otherwise great design. The key to successful storage is maintaining the image of the room while

providing the maximum amount of space necessary to easily stash away suitcases, purchases and any reminders of the transient nature of the guest's stay. As design hotels evolve, greater emphasis is put on imaginative planning, resulting in a rich and varied range of examples that demonstrate the ways and means of using any available storage space intelligently.

As an influential forerunner of today's new hotels, the Hempel in London is a seminal example of how to think laterally about storage. The impact of this hotel relies heavily – almost exclusively – on its strong, minimal design statement. As a result the emphasis placed on eradicating any visible clutter, clothes and baggage is correspondingly strong; hence the focus on storage in bedrooms. The idiosyncratic approach of the Hempel was to consider items of incidental furniture as viable and practical storage opportunities. The low table, for example, exceeds its ornamental function by providing discreet but roomy drawer space in its side panels. There are no protruding handles to disrupt the clean lines of the rest of the table, so it does not count as a functional object that needs to be hidden, and yet the redundant space beneath has been exploited. It is perhaps not an entirely original idea,

Above left *The room with 'the waterworks' is a well-known attraction at the Portobello, London. A glorious contraption of copper pipes, taps and sprinkler has been soldered on to a Victorian claw-footed bath – which stands in the middle of the room on an island of marble tiles. The approach here is to accord the bath a starring role, not relegate it to the wings.*
Above right *A revolving door panel in a suite at the Ace, Seattle, means the bathroom is seamlessly concealed from the main room; going in and out becomes a game even grown-ups enjoy.*
Opposite *Guests at the TriBeCa Grand, New York, can catch up on world news or the latest financial forecasts, as all bathrooms are equipped with a miniature TV screen.*

since it draws on Eastern traditions of design that dictate economical use of space, but its application in this context was groundbreaking.

As lifestyles evolve, the types of storage space required for a hotel bedroom must keep abreast of popular demand. Traditional allocations of vertical hanging space and drawers for clothes are no longer sufficient. The other necessary equipment that the modern traveller has in tow, such as laptops or mobile phones, must also have a designated or possible home.

Bathing beauty

The hotel bathroom, no longer the isolated and utilitarian space it once was, has been reinvented as a pampering zone adjacent to the bedroom. This new identity has forced designers of the new hotel to face the tricky ergonomic challenge of creating a room that delivers optimum comfort, performance and hygiene in an unusual and interesting way. The bathroom is most usefully considered as an extension of the style and design treatment of the bedroom itself, although the designer must remain acutely aware of the danger of overcomplicating what is essentially a functional adjunct to the bedroom itself.

The shape and size of bathrooms tend to remain more consistent than those of bedrooms but a wide variety of modern design treatments of the bath, shower, lavatory, basin and vanity areas are evident in the new hotel style.

The guestrooms at Babington House in Somerset, for example, have been designed in such a way that the layout reflects the hotel's easy-going version of rustic chic. This is particularly true in the treatment of the bathrooms. A sturdy, freestanding bathtub is positioned right at the foot of the platform bed, allowing guests to soak in a light, bright environment, where the funky white furniture and long, flowing curtains are illuminated by large windows on all sides.

The Portobello in London opts for a more novelty-driven approach, in keeping with its quirky, rather eccentric design statement. For example, one of the rooms eschews the banal modern shower unit, offering instead a gleaming extravaganza of exposed copper pipes and taps towering above the bath.

Integrating bathroom and bedroom

Finding a solution to the problem of how to integrate the bathroom into the bedroom space in a stylish way requires imaginative thought. It is not enough for the two rooms to complement each other in terms of their individual design; they must also work together as separate spaces. The new hotel has introduced a variety of methods to ensure that the bathroom remains accessible without being intrusive.

One of the most interesting examples of well-thought-out integration can be admired at the Ace in Seattle. The revolving mirror-door panel in the wall of one of the hotel's suites pivots on a central axis to allow the guest entry to the bathroom. The design is both practical and fun; it is also an intriguing and ingenious solution to the problem of how to organize the bedroom and the bathroom in such a way that they are conveniently linked to one another but remain totally separate at the same time.

Flushed with technology

The use of technology in the new hotel bathroom has increased markedly in recent years. Hotels such as the TriBeCa

Above *The sturdy timber floors and solid, minimal furnishings in the bedrooms of the Prince, Melbourne, enhance rather than detract from the original character of the old art-deco establishment. Nonetheless, this is a hotel with bespoke tailoring that is designed to fit the sassy modernist like a glove. Distinctive wicker lampshades recur not only in bedrooms and bathrooms but also in corridors, acting as a unifying motif. Added visual pleasure comes from the way in which, as the light is diffused between the woven strips, it casts sunray patterns on the wall behind.*

Above right *A smattering of designer furniture – such as these classic Jacobsen Egg chairs – in both the guestrooms and public areas of the Prince confirm its hip credentials. Where possible, architect Allan Powell has made maximum use of natural light to illuminate designer Paul Hecker's interiors; at midday the brilliance of the Australian sun can be filtered by adjusting the venetian blinds. Although the guestrooms present an atmosphere of carefully staged restraint, the now-expected luxury elements have not been omitted.*

Grand in New York or London's One Aldwych, for example, provide guests with mini TV monitors in the bathroom. This is an interesting development, as it redefines the bathroom as an area of the new hotel that deserves the same recognition and requisite technology as the bedroom. It is also a concession to the lifestyle of the modern hotel guest who may value the chance to catch up with the day's news or financial bulletins while shaving or showering first thing in the morning.

Seduction scenes

More and more, the new hotel is offering a theatrical experience to its customers and, as in the theatre, lighting is an important tool in this process. The bedroom can be considered centre stage in the overall production and it is in this particular area that the issue of lighting is most complex. Bedroom lighting must be versatile, sensual, flattering and functional, while giving maximum control to the customer.

The provision of natural light is a necessity for the bedroom. It may be controlled and diffused through the use of sheer drapes and full-length curtains, or even blocked out completely with blackout blinds, but it must still be available. Artificial light must also be easily controlled and manipulated. The tactical positioning of different lamps and the use of dimmer switches are easy ways of achieving flexible combinations of lighting.

Bedroom lighting breaks down into two basic categories: ambient lighting and task lighting. Ambient lighting is confined to the background, whereas task lighting caters for focused

'the contemporary hotel bedroom must establish a degree of consumer autonomy. Guests must have some control over their private environment. One increasingly common example of this is in-room technology.'

activities like reading or working. Task lighting should be stylish, it should not overrun the rest of the bedroom and it should be easily accessible and directed.

Carefully considered lighting can also be used to highlight various design features around the room or to create a certain mood, such as a ceiling light trained on the freshly turned-down bed or a desk light left on to make the room seem more inviting last thing at night.

Traditionally the lighting in hotel bathrooms has lacked detailed thought. The most common error is to light the bathroom too brightly but new hotels tend to confine bathroom lighting to a simple, discreet light above the vanity unit, which still has sufficient power (without the glare) to illuminate the rest of the room. Alternatively, a diffused overhead light or individual lamps may illuminate the bathroom as a whole, with highlights or spots subtly picking out the vanity area.

The office on the move

Business travel is a prevailing fact of modern hotel life, so the contemporary hotel bedroom must carry a number of extra facilities, which need to be simply and elegantly incorporated into the overall design.

The best way to tackle the question of sockets, modem and PC plug-ins and other office technology is to locate them at desk level or preferably to incorporate facilities associated with the business centre into the room itself. This might take the form of PC and Internet software integrated into the entertainment unit or, more commonly, fax machine, voicemail

and direct telephone lines as standard facilities. The Great Eastern Hotel in the City of London excels at this.

Privacy is, of course, a fundamental issue in the design of the hotel bedroom but links to the outside world also need to be available if desired. Cheaper and more widely available communications technology, particularly email and video-conferencing, has meant that it is now a viable option for many hotels to install these kinds of facilities as standard in bedrooms – a situation that would have been unthinkable only ten years ago. The resulting breed of twenty-first-century hotel is therefore able to be more flexible and offer a more targeted service to its guests by allowing them a greater degree of autonomy and independence.

Entertaining extras

The Westbourne in London's Notting Hill is one such gadget-conscious new hotel. Each of the 20 bedrooms is equipped with a wide-screen, plasma TV offering DVD, as well as full cable and internet access. Portable computers and fax machines are also available and even the 24-hour room service can be ordered electronically.

Technologically aware hotel group W Hotels was among the first to provide in-room internet access via the standard TV and entertainment unit. More recent ventures, such as the TriBeCa Grand in New York, have sought to refine the concept by offering better internet connectivity via high-speed ports, flexible control through wireless keyboards and greater range through multifunctional fax/copier/scanner units. Equally, business hotels such as the Regent Wall Street or the Avalon (both in New York) anticipate the needs of their corporate guests by equipping all bedrooms with speakerphones, cordless handsets and other trappings of today's office environment.

Similarly, the XV Beacon in Boston provides guests with ten business cards printed with the hotel's name and address upon arrival. The idea is to help its customers feel established in their new temporary office as soon as they have arrived. The fact that each room has three telephones (including one mobile to which messages can be forwarded from the room telephones) probably helps as well.

The Ritz-Carlton in Atlanta has taken this coddling approach one step further with the ultimate solution to its business guests' needs, in the form of a 24-hour technology butler. The butler is on call throughout the day and night and will eagerly apply his technological expertise to the task of mending a broken laptop or supplying frequently forgotten or misplaced items such as adapters or telephone cords.

The application of technology in the new hotel is not necessarily confined to boosting business facilities or creating labour-saving options for guests. There is also an aesthetic element at work. The guestrooms at One Aldwych in London, for example, have a switch located near the door that enables guests to inform the cleaning staff either that they do not want to be disturbed or that they wish the room to be cleaned. In the final analysis, this device is probably no more useful than the old-fashioned double door-handle signs that are still used

Above left As Cologne is one of Germany's main financial centres, the Wasserturm is acutely attuned to the needs of the twenty-first-century business traveller. Its guestrooms meet these with typical Andrée Putman flair, the curves and softness of a velvet chair balancing the hard angularity of lightbox-style desktop and lamp in a consummate case of opposites attract.
Above right The TriBeCa Grand, New York, meets the needs of its business travellers in its guestrooms with up-to-the-minute internet consoles that have chic, user-friendly keyboards free of unsightly wires.

in most hotels. But by creating a slick, technological alternative to the old-fashioned methodology, this hotel is setting itself apart as a sophisticated, modern hotel that is specifically targeting a twenty-first-century clientele who are utterly at ease with modern technology.

Personal services

There is no substitute for the personal touch, however, particularly when it is delivered in a spirit that is in keeping with the overall design message of the hotel. At the Loews Miami Beach Hotel, for example, guests are able to summon the bartender to their room in order for him to mix their desired cocktail on site. The service does not come cheap but, in an age of technological showboating in the hotel industry, this deftly repackaged butler concept has a novelty that is entirely suited to the new hotel.

the **urban** hotel

6

the urban revolution

'The new hotel must take a progressive, proactive stance and aim to stimulate the urban dweller by pinpointing emerging lifestyle trends while they are still at an embryonic stage.'

Above *The Mercer, at the very heart of New York's SoHo, is a mecca for the fashion designers, photographers, stylists, advertising creatives and other trendsetters who have migrated to this now-hip zip code.*

Opposite *The Adelphi, Melbourne, has an enviable address in the city's most avant-garde street, among the major art galleries, and a short walk away from nightclubs, theatres and the designer shops of Bourke Street.*

The new urban hotel has certain specific characteristics that set it apart from a traditional townhouse hotel. They are both located in metropolitan areas but the contemporary urban hotel is competing for a more sophisticated and elusive market, not simply cornering transient residential trade. Of course, all hotels offer a traditional service to their guests, but the new hotel also strives to extend the sphere of its attraction and generate new business from new markets by adopting a specific design approach. These new markets are tied in with fashion, social trends and shifts in business manners and protocol, so it is no longer enough for the hotel simply to blend in with its urban setting. The new hotel must take a more aggressive, proactive stance and aim to stimulate the urban dweller by pinpointing emerging lifestyle trends while they are still at an embryonic stage. And it is the role of the designer to create exactly the right conditions in which those lifestyle trends may take hold.

In some senses the urban hotel spearheads the evolution of the new hotel. Because of its complex and cosmopolitan setting it is forced to adapt to a level of sophistication that suits its more discerning urban audience. It becomes a one-stop shop: not just a hotel but also a destination bar, a restaurant, a health club or spa and neutral territory for business meetings, both formal and casual. Inevitable competition from nearby rivals to these stand-alone elements

of the urban hotel puts extra pressure on the designer to find ever more ingenious ways of both enticing passing trade and winning the loyalty of the local business fraternities.

I'll drink to that

Location is the first important consideration for the operator of the urban hotel. Areas that offer easy access to the main business district, as well as shopping, theatre, restaurants and nightlife, would be an obvious choice. The new hotel often tends to bypass the obvious choice of location, however, and opt for an area that is a kind of design statement in itself. The SoHo Grand and the TriBeCa Grand in New York, the Hempel in London or the Gastwerk in Hamburg are all examples of urban hotels that have strayed from the main strip and set up shop in unlikely or bold locations. Hotels such as these have managed to spot niche trends and lifestyles, such as the birth of loft-conversion apartments in SoHo, and capitalize on them before they hit the mainstream or else just when they are on the cusp of mass media exposure.

By definition the urban hotel is located in a busy, densely populated area and the implication is that it allows easy access to all the advantages of urban living. But the contemporary spin on this image is a hotel that not only offers a prime urban location but also lays claim to having the area's best bar, restaurant and A-list social scene right on the premises. Traditionally the public perception of hotel amenities, most of all bars and restaurants, has never been good but the new hotel has banished such preconceptions of mediocrity for ever. The myth to be exploded was the idea that hotel dining is *de facto* a dull, stodgy experience.

Marriage of convenience

Grand hotels such as the Ritz have always known the advantages of teaming up with big-name chefs, like Auguste Escoffier, and they have deservedly profited from their foresight. It was only in the latter part of the twentieth century, however, that the new, less established hotels, spurred on by the advent of the celebrity chef, began to cash in on this ruse as well. This is a phenomenon that first took hold in cities across the world but it soon spread to more rural areas. Famous chefs such as Jean-Georges Vongerichten (notably at the Berkeley in London and the Mercer in New York) and Jean-Louis Palladin (at the Time hotel in New York and the Rio Suites in Las Vegas) have played a seminal part in putting some of the world's top new hotels on the map. Similarly, the recruitment of high-profile names to a hitherto unremarkable

kitchen, such as Pierre Koffmann's migration to the Berkeley in London, has helped to reinstate some of the world's grandest hotels as serious players in the twenty-first-century market.

Cultivating kudos

Pioneers of the lounge-bar culture that swept the 1990s into a frenzy of urban posturing, such as Dick Bradsell, have also played their part in promoting the new hotel. Early destination bars were instrumental in drawing a celebrity crowd and nurturing an A-list clientele, achieving the hoped-for result of bestowing invaluable kudos on the hotel on top of establishing the bar's reputation as a slick, stand-alone drinking venue.

But all performers require a stage, and the design approach of the bars and restaurants of the new hotel has to be

Above *The Rum Bar in Asia de Cuba, the fusion restaurant at St Martins Lane, London, boasts a dazzling display of 120 different rums. Philippe Starck's tables are as directional as the designer cocktails and provide elegant perches for pre-prandial drinks.*
Opposite *David Collins' refurbishment of the art-deco bar at Claridge's, London, has created a cool destination bar in this venerable institution, giving it cult status among the style cognoscenti.*

consistent both with the overall tone of the establishment and with the specific market and lifestyle aspirations of the consumer. The balance is to create a bar or restaurant that fits with the rest of the hotel without resorting to a homogenized, blanket design manifesto that robs the area of its individuality. The desired effect is that of a jigsaw, where all of the pieces fit together thanks to common design features – such as the materials or the quality of the finishes – while retaining an individual style.

St Martins Lane in London, for example, offers the Asia de Cuba restaurant, the more affordable Saint M, the Sea Bar and the Rum Bar (see p. 107). Each has a different price option, design and identity but there are certain common themes, such as the choice of furniture, the lighting effects, the neutral colour palette, the stylish accessories and the attention to detail. It is also important to notice that all of the bar and restaurant venues at St Martins Lane are immediately accessible via the lobby. The design of the space allows them to remain distinct from but definitely joined to the hotel at the same time.

Access all areas

The TriBeCa Grand in New York has taken this principle one step further by having no formal restaurant in the hotel as such; instead it has converted its atrium lounge into what it terms a movable feast. The design of this area incorporates a variety of low lounge furniture and café-style tables and chairs that can be rearranged in a number of different configurations, thus allowing for a maximum of flexibility in terms of the character and functionality of the space. The design is intended to suit the many different needs of the modern traveller, and is summed up in the hotel's literature as an environment that enables a guest whose appetite is still in another time zone to have breakfast when meeting a friend who is ready for dinner.

Similarly, the Grand Hyatt in Berlin has a lobby that allows access to several eating and drinking areas, the most prestigious of which is the Dietrich bistro. Spaniard Rafael Moneo and Swiss Hannes Wettstein are the team behind the lobby design, which features an unusual glass ceiling element akin in shape and function to an enormous crystal. The prismatic structure illuminates the lobby with both daylight and artificial light and makes for an interesting, attractive junction between the various gastronomic options that the hotel offers to residents and non-residents alike.

Above Those who want the lowdown on the next big thing flock to the Mercer Kitchen in the hotel's basement: it is famously where SoHo's media hotshots share a sun-dried tomato.
Opposite The two-storey rooftop Felix restaurant crowns the Peninsula, Hong Kong. Every ingredient, from chairs to china, was designed by Philippe Starck, resulting in the very pinnacle of elite eateries.

Brand new

Branding a hotel bar or restaurant can be problematic, since both traditionally have been the victim of some major (and often thoroughly deserved) negative preconceptions. On the whole the new hotel has chased away the image of the overpriced hotel restaurant that preys on a captive audience or the rarely used hotel bar that remains out of touch and unresponsive to the rest of the market. For the most part this has been achieved through an original and strong design message, combined with coherent and, above all, subtle branding.

Branding is a term that should be interpreted very loosely in the context of the new hotel bar or restaurant; a more accurate way of describing the process might be fine tuning. This may be defined as the ability to import a successful outside formula that will blend with the image of the hotel and suit the clientele, or it may involve the harder task of creating a new product for the hotel that synchronizes with the design statement of the rest of the establishment.

Making space

A limitation on space is obviously a prime concern for the designer of the urban hotel. The luxury of spacious grounds and gardens is sacrificed in favour of the buzzing urban location. The problem of where to site swimming pools, tennis courts,

courtyards and gardens follows from this. The premium on space means that the designer of the new urban hotel must find a viable way of working successfully within those confines without disrupting the image and design identity of the hotel.

The Adelphi in Melbourne is a good example of how the application of a little lateral thinking and a fair degree of ingenuity can resolve this kind of problem. Now a Melbourne landmark, the glass-bottomed rooftop pool at the Adelphi forms a very strong design statement. The pool juts out over the edge of the building, the brightly coloured girders that support it visible from street level. It is an obvious talking point with both visitors and passers-by, but the real triumph of the pool at the Adelphi is the fact that not only is it a clever solution to the spatial restrictions on designing an urban hotel, it is also a prominent design feature in its own right. Its situation among

Opposite and above The cantilevered, glass-bottomed lap pool extending from the roof of the Adelphi, Melbourne, proclaims to passers-by eight storeys below on Flinders Lane that here is a hotel that dares to be different. A celebrated addition to the city skyline, it demonstrates the designers' determination to go to any lengths – even to defy gravity – to provide guests with an urban oasis.

the surrounding rooftops lends the pool area a surreal quality, and guests are invited to a secret eyrie or oasis of calm high above street level where they can relax on the terrace or take cooling dips in the pool.

The garden created at the Hempel in London, however, is not particularly user-friendly. The strong emphasis on aesthetics reflects the nature of the city and the hotel's clientele. In other words, London, unlike Melbourne, is not a sunny and breezy getaway destination and those who are likely to visit a hotel such as the Hempel are sure to have an interest in the world of design and more likely to appreciate form over function.

The Hôtel Costes in Paris provides yet another example of how the garden of a modern urban hotel can overcome the limitations of minimal space to achieve maximum impact. The courtyard at the Costes is not immediately apparent from the street and its seclusion allows the designer to incorporate the restaurant deftly into this outside space. As a result, the decorative nineteenth-century Orientalist façade of the building encloses a courtyard that not only adds an inner dimension of space to the structure of the hotel itself but also forms part of the restaurant. This section is exposed during the summer months and can be covered by a retractable roof in winter, which is an effective device in an urban setting, since the opportunity for creating an added sense of space and freedom in the interior design is always available but not mandatory.

The pursuit of beauty

An integral part of the new urban hotel is its spa or health and beauty facilities. The stress and rigours of living in a city mean that this kind of oasis of calm and relaxation is held particularly dear by the clientele of the urban hotel. By definition the target market of the urban hotel are professional, independent individuals who live at a fast pace; it is therefore obvious that they will need to be able to wind down and relax at the end of the day. The designer must consider the fact that many of those who use the health and beauty facilities of the urban hotel are not going to be its guests. Like the bar and restaurant, the hotel spa in any new urban hotel is a stand-alone destination and it must be designed with that in mind, as many of its non-resident clients will treat it as a private health club.

The Agua spa at the Sanderson in London (see p. 113) is a case in point. The area is divided up by billowing white curtain partitions, creating an ambience of ethereal calm and relieving the senses of any unnecessary stimulation. This is an environment that has been devised as a kind of express check-

Left *At the Atoll in Heligoland, Germany, the pool plays a central role in the hotel's design statement. Sited below the lobby, it forms a tranquil blue haven viewed through a series of circular windows cut into the lobby floor.*

Opposite *The Agua spa in the Sanderson, London is a 30,500-metre split-level sanctuary created by Philippe Starck. Curtains of luminous white voile soothe jet-lagged clients into a state of angelic bliss.*

in to a state of peace and relaxation, hinting at a Hollywood dream sequence as customers drift through vast swathes of flowing white material *en route* to the spa. The dreamlike effect is enhanced by the ever-present sound of running water, the source of which is a peaceful water feature that dominates the waiting area. At every stage of the process customers' expectations are confounded by innovative design. The glass walls of the steamroom, for instance, are constantly changing colour, illuminating the permanent film of condensation that conceals the interior.

Spa culture

The aim of this kind of design spa, just like Schrager's Agua spa at the Delano in Miami, is to nurture a culture of its own, an identity that is separate from the hotel. And design is the key to success. Design hotels around the world eschew the commonly accepted idea of a bolt-on gym or fitness centre and try instead to create something that is impressive in its own right and has a tangible aesthetic appeal of its own.

The top-floor swimming pool and fitness area at the Grand Hyatt in Berlin are highlights of the hotel's design message. Rafael Moneo and Hannes Wettstein have this time created an angular, modern environment with spectacular views over the city. Low ceilings lend an intimate, cosseting feel to the space and broad expanses of window allow the daylight to flood in and give customers the feeling of being suspended above – and therefore completely removed from – the noise and pollution of the city. The showers, which have a bare, rustic simplicity that recalls the scrubbed, pristine quality of a Swiss mountain spa, serve to reinforce this message.

The design of the Rock Spa at the Hard Rock in Las Vegas takes into account the lifestyle and aspirations of its hip clientele by providing them with a funky but fundamentally chilled-out area in which to detox and prepare for the next round of partying. The natural brickwork and stonework shift the focus on to the restorative, cleansing qualities of sauna, steamroom, massage and hydrotherapy. The location does, however, overlook the hotel's pool – the hub of the action – and the Rock Spa is therefore made to seem easily accessible. The designer is seducing guests with the dual appeal of a sanctuary set apart from the rather frenetic pace of bars, nightclubs and rock concerts but at the same time still in the thick of the action.

It is also imperative that the new urban hotel ensures that the entrance of its spa is attractive and alluring; it must be the kind of space that seems both exclusive and welcoming. One example of this might be the reception of the health club at One Aldwych in London. The cool blue glass of the counter is warmly lit to create a welcoming glow but the quilted steel panelling opposite suggests that the design-conscious manifesto that characterizes the rest of the hotel will be upheld here, too. This impression is later justified by the ambitious swimming pool, for instance, which favours clean and minimal lines with a delicate spiral staircase and sturdy industrial girders.

Make business a pleasure

It is undeniably the case that, because of its location, the urban hotel has a business edge over other new hotels. More remote hotels simply cannot compete (on a business level) with urban hotels, despite the advent of sophisticated video-conferencing equipment and in-room facilities such as email and internet access. One of the main strengths of the urban hotel, then, is that it can often offer an alternative office space in the heart of a major business centre. With this in mind, the designer must create meeting and conference spaces that are tailored to the high-octane worlds of twenty-first-century business and finance but at the same time retain the sex appeal of the new hotel.

It is worth considering what kind of business people are the most frequent users of new hotels. The majority tend to be from the media, film, advertising, PR and other professions looking for high-impact glamour for product launches and publicity-driven events. The designer must therefore be aware of the target audience, their expectations and, most importantly, their aspirations. For this reason the hitherto neglected appendage of the business centre or conference room has been re-examined by the new hotel and transformed into an exciting and stimulating space. Conducting business in hotels has thus ceased to be confined to tedious conventions and stale presentations; it is now the realm of corporate sex appeal, with designs to match.

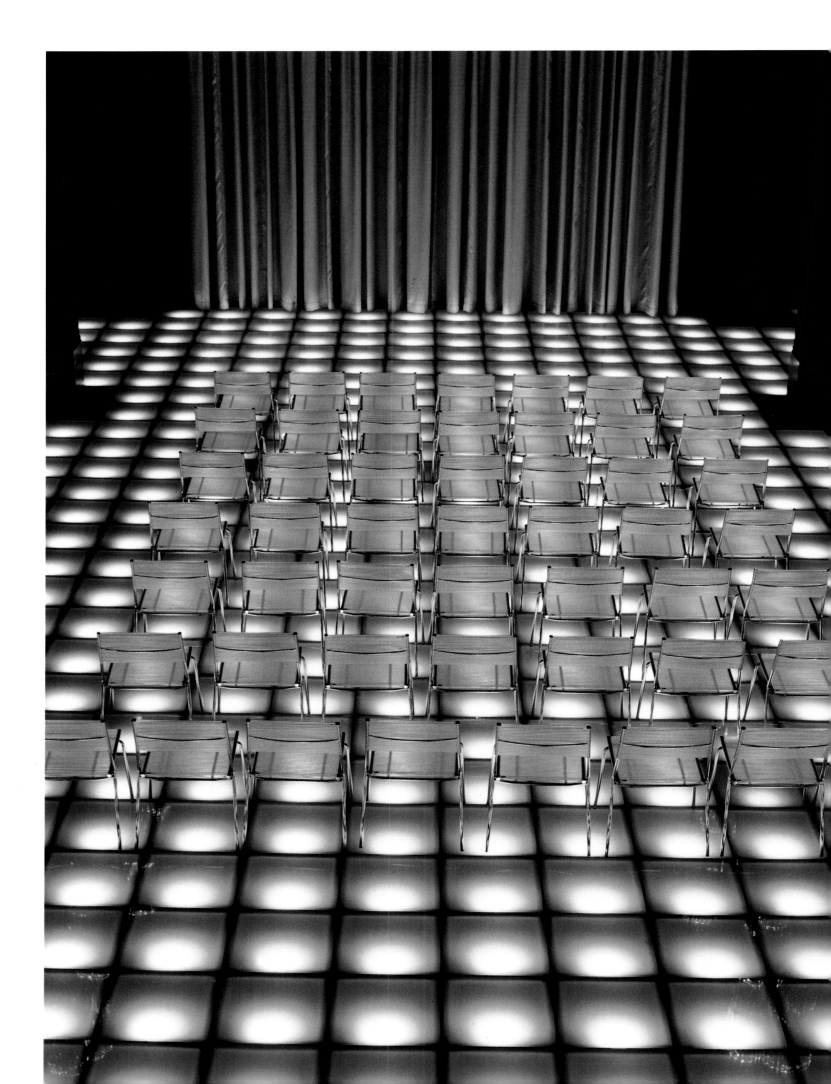

From an architectural viewpoint, one of the most extraordinary conference centres of any new hotel is that of Le Meridien Lingotto in Turin. This cantilevered conference pod has been designed as a totally modern think-bubble, suspended out on a limb and flooded with natural light through its glass walls. Instead of an anonymous, soporific auditorium design, the Lingotto is presenting its guests with a challenging and stimulating environment in which to work.

Similar in principle to the design of its restaurant area, the meeting and conference facility that the TriBeCa Grand in New York offers its guests could just as easily morph into a reception area or state-of-the-art screening room. Larry Brogdanow – the man behind a number of acclaimed New York restaurant interiors – designed this multipurpose arena, using colours and materials that challenge the dull conventions of theatre-style designs. The curved backs of the chairs hint at the fun, frivolous mood of a sports stadium rather than a stuffy business venue, while the corded plush upholstery, in tones of rust, plum, moss and gold, suggests a serious, elegant side to the room.

Exclusively business

Although location is important, it is not the only consideration for the modern business hotel, and properties such as the Avalon in New York win their clientele through a tightly targeted approach. The Avalon is an exclusively business hotel and its facilities have been designed with this in mind. A free glass of champagne for guests on their arrival suggests this is a hotel that is aiming to rival establishments such as the Regent Wall Street, and spacious rooms offering free internet access and two-line speaker telephones confirm this initial impression. The design also incorporates the kind of luxury materials flaunted by the Regent, such as Egyptian cotton bedlinen and marble bathrooms.

Also with the needs of the modern business traveller firmly at the forefront of their minds, the design team behind the Holiday Inn Express in Cleveland, USA, has conjured a bespoke atmosphere for a different segment of the market: the design-conscious businessman on a budget. Although this

Opposite A futuristic forum of space and light, the conference room at the Dorint am Gendarmenmarkt, Berlin, is set for the twenty-first century. The glass floortiles, preserved from the 1980s, make a striking stage for aluminium and plastic-weave chairs designed by Pierre-Antonio Bancina.

hotel is part of a chain, the experience it offers is unique. The building was converted from a bank and the designers have retained some impressive marble pillars in the lobby, as well as conserving the high ceilings in the bedrooms. Similarly, Edinburgh City Travel Inn has slipped the bonds of its budget category and come up with an impressive design manifesto of cool colours and slick, clean lines, both outside and in.

Easy access

The fact that location is an important characteristic of the modern urban hotel has already been mentioned and this is particularly true of the business hotel. The most significant business hotel to open in New York in recent years, for example, is the Regent Wall Street. This is the establishment that has resuscitated the beautiful nineteenth-century

'the designer must create meeting and conference spaces that are tailored to the high-octane worlds of twenty-first-century business and finance but at the same time retain the sex appeal of the new hotel.'

Merchants' Exchange building on the city's premier financial strip. The reason it is so notable is that it is the first hotel to have opened on Wall Street.

The site is very grand and the architectural legacy of McKim, Mead and White's famous restoration of the building in 1907 is a designer's dream. A wealth of Renaissance features has survived from its days as a banking hall and the vocabulary of the interior design recalls traditional Italian style with sumptuous mixes of velvets, chenille and silk damask, punctuated by rich colours and heavy marble. In short, the design had to be strong enough to support such a heavyweight location – and it is.

The meeting rooms at the Regent Wall Street make the most of the original soaring architecture. The retained features comprise 1,115 square metres (12,000 square feet) of grey Botticini marble floors and walls, Corinthian columns and a central elliptical ceiling that boasts the largest Wedgwood panels in the world. But, far from seeming over the top, the design is entirely in keeping with the hotel's Wall Street setting. It is only logical that, even in the midst of a new hotel, which makes every concession to technology and modern travel trends, the business facilities should be unashamedly unrestrained and grandiose in appearance.

the **getaway** hotel

7

modern sanctuaries

'The task of the designer of the getaway hotel is to create surroundings that lure guests away from the frenetic rhythms of their daily lives.'

One of the few luxuries that even the busy super-rich cannot afford is time. It is because of the precious nature of this commodity that the new hotel has made a business out of maximizing the time that is available to contemporary travellers. Hotel operators have realized that the most effective way of boosting the quality of the time available to their guests is to create an environment, a portfolio of treatments and activities, and a level of service that allow busy people to unwind fast. So the task of the designer of the getaway hotel is to create surroundings that lure guests away from the frenetic rhythms of their daily lives, lulling them into a temporary world that is purged of deadlines, pressures of work and the stresses of modern life. In short, the aim is to make time stand still.

It is also important to remember, when considering the merits of any getaway hotel, that it must, by definition, be a self-contained product. That is not to say that the building should imprison its guests; the opposite is usually the case. For example, the setting of the getaway hotel is often just as

Left and opposite *At first sight, the Amanjena resort, Morocco, looks almost like a film set, but this Moorish mirage is wondrously real. Within sight of the souks and minarets of Marrakesh, the complex lies amid palms and old olive trees, forming a luxurious refuge set around an ancient irrigation pool or bassin. Its pavilions and* maisons *are the last word in decadence, equipped with minibars, TVs, bathrooms of green Moroccan marble, a* minzah *(gazebo) and a personal butler.*

spectacular as – if not more so than – the design of the building itself. But the point in this case is that the getaway hotel is not a base from which to visit other places; it is an experience that should be discrete. Without the sense of isolation and seclusion the whole concept of getting away or escaping evaporates, leaving nothing more interesting than the next resort or holiday villa. Hence the new hotel has manufactured a one-stop shop for both physical and mental rejuvenation, and the design and the services on offer should reflect this down to the last detail.

Got to get away

More than any other type of new hotel, the modern getaway destination trades on its location. Environment is a key factor in creating stress – traffic jams, rainy streets and noisy offices being some obvious examples – so it is only logical that it should play a pivotal role in eliminating stress as well. Exotic locations, remote hideaways and elegant townhouse addresses are the kinds of places to which the twenty-first-century customer wants to flee. This is a competitive market and one that caters to all levels of

demand, but the new getaway hotel separates itself from the rest with one simple distinction: design. The architecture, landscaping and design of a getaway hotel are more important to its success than any other factors. In a modern market where guests can book in for a massage at any hotel fitness centre, there needs to be an X factor, a defining characteristic of the quality experience.

X factor

Aman Resorts' first property in Africa, Amanjena in Morocco, is a prime example of a hotel that has identified and included that X factor successfully. The name means peaceful paradise, which could in any other circumstances be a risible cliché, but the Hollywood splendour and the ambitious scale of this project fit the confident claims of its branding. It looks as if it has been built as a set for a Fritz Lang film, with its grand, opulent interiors and the Moorish twists and turns in the architecture. It is located at an oasis, the Atlas mountain range carves up the horizon and palm fronds and olive trees provide the shady corners. It is almost biblical in tone and, as a result, about as far removed from the cut and thrust of modern life as it is possible to get. The

accommodation is divided into pavilions with private walled gardens, their open fireplaces, towering ceilings and king-sized beds giving them luxurious appeal year round. The seven two-storey *maisons* come with plunge pools and an extra bedroom. The complex is artfully laid out to fit around 60 square metres (645 square feet) of water in an ancient irrigation pool that acts as a kind of aquatic central square. The predominating colours are those of the surrounding sun-scorched territories – a fiery range of reds, oranges and baked browns – and the tiled floors, pillars and tall windows ensure that the buildings never subside into gloominess. The identity of the hotel has been very carefully crafted. The presiding Moroccan motifs, the open-air courtyards

and the steamy hammams reflect the ethnicity and history of the location but this never becomes a preoccupation. Even the bespoke walking tours to Berber villages or into the mountains are very much levelled at the modern, discerning traveller. The emphasis is on choice and *laissez-faire* – indeed many guests never get further than their gardens – but the objective of providing concentrated doses of relaxation (if required) remains keenly focused in the minds of the staff. More importantly still, the palatial tone of the surroundings is a contemporary take on exotic design that supplies just the right measure of escapism. A second and more extreme case of a hotel identifying and using the X factor, with design being employed to enhance the getaway

destination, is that of the Atelier sul Mare hotel in Sicily. It is the clearest possible illustration of how total design commitment and a spectacular location can be successfully combined to create a stimulating and relaxing retreat. The hotel is situated on the wild northeast coast of the island, with spectacular ocean views, yet what sets it apart from any of the other destinations in Sicily is the fact that each of its 40 rooms is being decorated in turn by a different artist from around the world.

In some senses this hotel represents the ultimate concession to the aesthetic curiosity of the modern traveller. The owner, Antonio Presti, intended the hotel to be a living art installation, where the design of each space is unique and guests can view any room. One room is clad entirely in red mud, with primitive furnishings and rough-hewn doorways that are intended as a tribute to Italian film director Pasolini's passion for the architecture of the Yemen. Another room by Chilean film director Raoul Ruiz, is shaped like a tower and has a retractable roof and revolving circular bed; a mini planetarium in other words. In another egg-shaped room called Nest, Paolo Icaro banishes any busy colours or clever gadgetry, opting instead for the purity of white surfaces and a quilt resembling swan's feathers.

Atelier is representative of the modern approach to the hotelier's art. It is no longer good enough just to establish guests in fabulous surroundings and leave them to their own devices; the new hotel also posits stimulation for the mind as an integral part of the antidote to the stresses and strains of twenty-first-century living. This kind of fantastical, almost dreamlike, setting is a direct response to the evolving needs of the modern traveller, who has rejected the pool bar and piña colada culture of more traditional getaway destinations and installed new icons of fashion and design in the search for the ultimate luxury retreat.

The design statement

There is another common approach to the design of the new getaway hotel that is at the opposite pole of thought from the contrived interiors of hotels like Atelier sul Mare. This is best described as the residential influence. In design terms the word residential roughly translates as a traditional emphasis, a vocabulary of design whose prime objective is to evoke the idyllic home from home. To achieve this effect a strong design statement is required. The designer needs to instil a sure and confident character into the surroundings; it must be a look that is totally lacking in pretension, so as to reassure customers that this is a place where they can really relax and be themselves.

The most conspicuous example of this theory put successfully into practice must be Chris Blackwell's Island Outposts group of hotels. Strewn across the Caribbean, these isolated yet modern resorts have engendered more than just a cult following; they seem to embody a complete philosophy of organic architecture and residential influence in hotel design.

One of the group's legendary resorts, Strawberry Hill in Jamaica, exemplifies every aspect of the Blackwell credo of new hotel design. The accommodations have been etched out

Above *When Goldeneye, Jamaica, was home to Ian Fleming he would bathe naked at sunrise in the crystal-clear waters. Today guests of the Island Outpost resort can still appreciate why in 1956 Sir Anthony Eden wrote: 'The bathing, the beach, the seclusion, the size of the grounds were all just perfect to enjoy and be concealed.'*

Opposite *Rustic, locally crafted furniture contributes to the lush, tropical atmosphere at Strawberry Hill, Jamaica.*

of the landscape on the site of a former great house just outside Kingston. The design is most definitely organic in its penchant for the pitched roofs and fretwork that are so deeply characteristic of the area, along with the fact that the rough-hewn landscaping of the garden has preserved some rather awkwardly positioned trees and verges that prevent the whole from seeming pre-planned. It seems to have evolved naturally into a resort over a protracted period of time. However, concessions to the luxury-hungry modern traveller are also evident at Strawberry Hill. The oversailing roofs, for instance, are not so much a nod to the indigenous contours of Jamaican design but more of a practical consideration, enabling guests to enjoy an alfresco aperitif even during a tropical cloudburst.

Clocking off, gearing up

On the northern coast of the island, in Oracabessa, Blackwell has created another resort that captures the spirit of the place. It has a sense of adventure and the kind of down-tempo lifestyle that such a picturesque and climatically suitable location naturally suggests: the place is Goldeneye, the former home of Ian Fleming.

Blackwell had something of a headstart in terms of imbuing these two resorts with a residential mood: he once lived at Strawberry Hill and he used Goldeneye as a holiday retreat long before it was opened to the public. The conversion of both has transformed them into twenty-first-century resorts but the breezy casualness of both staff and decor are pivotal to their success. The guest quarters at Strawberry Hill, for instance, are decorated with furniture and fittings designed by local craftsmen, while the showers at Goldeneye are open-air jets of water in thick bamboo cages with luxury toiletries perched on crude pebble shelving.

What is important from a design viewpoint, however, is maintaining the balance between the rugged, organic elements and the luxury, pampering touches. The wooden villas at Strawberry Hill, for example, may look as if they are truly part of a primitive outpost, dislocated from modern civilization, but one visit to the resort's Aveda Concept Spa should assuage any doubts. The success of Island Outposts resorts is dependent on this ability to balance zeitgeist elements, such as state-of-the-art spa treatments, finest cotton sheets and funky updates on Jamaican cuisine, with the timeless organic design of the properties and the remoteness of the locations. Guests will discover satellite TV, VCRs and CD players secreted somewhere among the locally crafted furniture and artwork.

The youth market

Compass Point on the Bahamian island of Nassau represents another facet of the Island Outposts' portfolio, namely fun in the sun. Blackwell's background in the music industry (he founded Island Records) means that he is still tuned in to the aspirations of the youth market. Whiz kids are also looking for a remote getaway but one with more vibrancy and not so much of the sleepy charm of Strawberry Hill and Goldeneye.

Hence the bold primary colours and private beach scene of Compass Point. Each of the 18 huts, cottages and cabanas is splashed with vivid colours – turquoise, tangerine, teal, canary

Left *Huts at the Makalali Private Game Reserve, South Africa, epitomize ethnic luxe. An ethereal tent of mosquito netting hangs from Masai spears, while the individuality of rough-hewn walls and handmade furnishings has the highest cachet in today's mass-produced world.*

Opposite *At the Four Seasons resort in Jimbaran Bay, Bali, thatched hillside villas overlook a sparkling sea. Garden courtyards have private pools, incense perfumes the air and pebbled pathways give bare feet reflexology treatments.*

and cerise. Nightclubs and casinos are within easy access and, on their return, guests can throw open the louvred windows and look directly out on to the ocean.

Compass Point bears a greater similarity to the group's suite of hotels along Miami's South Beach than it does to the other classic getaway properties owned by Island Outposts, but it is significant because it represents a more happening side of the modern getaway market. One aspect that unites all these properties, however, is their location. In fact, a group such as Island Outposts deliberately conjures an image of far-flung seclusion just through its name and branding, an indication of just how far up the list of customer priorities location comes.

Cosmopolitan castaways

One of the group's more secluded resorts, Pink Sands on Harbour Island in the Bahamas, is a good illustration of exactly why location is considered such a priority. The resort's history makes it an interesting case study for the modern hotel designer. The site has existed as a hotel for nearly 50 years but it was only in 1995 that Barbara Hulanicki, designer for Island Outposts, revamped it. This therefore provides an opportunity to look at what distinguishes the new getaway hotel from its forebears. The

main factor certainly is not location, as the tiny Harbour Island has always drawn tourists to its exclusive pink sand beaches and crystal waters. Instead it is its eclectic design manifesto that nudges this resort into the contemporary arena, with wry modern interiors described by the designer as a Moroccan-Indian fantasy. Hulanicki was responsible for the design of the Marlin, Leslie and Cavalier hotels in Miami's South Beach, and it was these vibrant art-deco renovations that spearheaded the area's ascent into the heights of hotel fashion. But the concept behind Pink Sands is worlds away from the urban chic of South Beach.

The 25 cottages that comprise the resort are traditionally Bahamian in design, in keeping with the group's commitment to organic architecture. Equally, the gardens have a similar landscaped quality to those at Strawberry Hill and Compass Point (architect Stephen Haus designed all three). Yet the interiors are a departure from the kind of local arts and crafts that might be the natural choice. Oversized wooden Adirondack furniture inside (painted to match the pastel hues of the rooms) and East Indian teak furniture on the patios give a fresh and funky edge to the design. The floors are covered with rough-cut Italian marble and the tiles in the bathrooms have also been imported from Europe. All the materials have

been specifically chosen to bring a luxurious, sophisticated air to the castaway location.

The Caribbean-Asian fusion cooking in the two restaurants continues the exotic motif and helps to locate this far-flung destination in the glittering firmament of the new hotel. Here guests can enjoy shaved prosciutto and poached spiced pear served with local papaya, for example. The addition of a slick exercise studio is a key acknowledgment of the habits and obsessions of the busy modern customer. The bottom line is that, just like its urban counterpart, the new getaway hotel needs to keep its eye firmly fixed on the aspirations of its clientele. The sophisticated modern consumer needs more than just the allure of a fabulous destination.

Privacy please

The design of new hotels is almost always related to the specific requirements of the clientele and, in the case of the getaway destination, a major factor to be considered is how best to accommodate the independently minded traveller. The contemporary resort hotel must be designed with the customer's self-assured demands for privacy in mind. It is for this reason that accommodations often tend to take the form of bungalows, huts and cabanas or, at the very least, rooms with their own pool, patio or garden. The design statement should affirm the current trend towards privacy and exclusivity even within the confines of a modern resort, as modern travellers need to be accorded the requisite seclusion and independence to make them feel completely relaxed and in charge of their surroundings.

This element of empowerment can also be achieved through the design of the common areas of the hotel, which should aim to break down inhibitions by incorporating plenty of sheltered corners and ergonomic, casual seating. At Ariel Sands in Bermuda, for instance, guests are likely to happen upon low-slung hammocks that have been casually strung between a couple of likely trees in the garden leading down to the beach. Take it or leave it, the option is there.

Weather or not

Climate is clearly a consideration when attempting to contrive this kind of happy-go-lucky feel to a hotel. The Tamarindo in Mexico, for example, accommodates its guests in thatched palapa villas with open-air living and dining areas. Guests can breeze in and out as they please, but this kind of open-plan design approach would be impossible in a harsher climate. The fact that the Tamarindo is surrounded by 2,000 acres of privately owned rainforest undoubtedly has a bearing on the free-roaming feel of the place.

However, this effect can still be achieved even when space is limited, as in the case of the Casa Natalia, also in Mexico. This hotel does not have its own chunk of rainforest but good use has been made of the space that is available within the confines of the former eighteenth-century private residence. Rooms with private balconies or terraces are grouped around a palm-filled courtyard and in the evening the whole scene is illuminated by torches. Splashes of indigenous colour are evident in the various furnishings and fittings, and the sense of illusion, of pure escapism, is promoted by the theatricality of the design.

Escapism

Many new getaway hotels have successfully secured a portion of the eco-tourist dollar through their location in some of the world's most renowned areas of unspoilt natural beauty. Just such a place is the Al Maha Desert Resort in Dubai. The resort has been built in the style of a traditional Bedouin encampment and is set within 25 square kilometres (just over 9$\frac{1}{2}$ square miles) of desert conservation reserve. The location is unquestionably stunning, with the huge sky and the far-off prospect of the Hajar Mountains dominating the arid and dusty landscape.

Above right *At Devigarh Palace, India, guests are pampered in princely style, in keeping with the building's history. Wholly white rooms ease minds into meditative peace, while bodies are relaxed by a yoga teacher and Ayurvedic doctor.*

Right *An essential-oil massage at the Aveda spa prepares guests for siesta in a hammock at Strawberry Hill, Jamaica.*

Opposite *Al Maha, Dubai, is set around a desert oasis in a conservation area, with panoramic views of the Hajar Mountains. After a camel safari to spot Arabian oryx and rheem gazelle, mint tea is served in tentlike suites with rooms decorated in Bedouin splendour.*

The Al Maha Desert Resort is divided into suites, all of which have their own terrace and chilled plunge pool. The design is intended to blend in with the surroundings, mirroring the style of the traditional Bedouin tents, with their billowing canvas roofs that oversail the terrace and provide valuable shade. This imparts a make-believe quality to the site that provides guests with an added level of escapism – as though they are being given the chance to step into a completely unfamiliar and exotic way of life for the duration of their stay. Of course, the undesirable aspects of that primitive life have been richly westernized for the benefit of the twenty-first-century paying guest, as evidenced by the king-size baths, walk-in showers and, of course, room service.

100% organic

Another luxury resort that has taken a distinctively organic approach to the issues of design and layout is the Begawan Giri estate in Bali. The product of nine years' work, the five principal buildings of the resort have adopted elemental design motifs in order to make them blend in with their surroundings. The suites in the Clear Water residence, for example, have been constructed using solid, traditional materials, such as 150-year-old Javanese teak, and they are enhanced by the sound and spectacle of an elaborate water garden that lends a distinctly Zen note to the space. Similarly, the Sound of Fire residence has used novelty materials in its construction (in this case 1,200 tonnes/1,180 tons of stone imported from the island of Sumba). The roofs are

thatched and the furniture is upholstered in tribal cloth but the most extraordinary feature is a primeval fire-pit located at the edge of the pool. This is a dramatic design statement whose purpose is to remind guests of the elements of nature and to symbolize their return to a closer contact with what the brochure describes as its primal power.

The other residences advertise the various merits of wind, earth and forest through the use of similar architectural and design devices. In a sense, then, Begawan Giri is an example of a new getaway destination that has been so carefully and thoroughly integrated into its natural surroundings that this concept of a oneness with nature becomes the main thrust of its design message and, indeed, its advertising and branding.

Rock 'n' roll coasters

At the opposite end of the spectrum of contemporary retreats, however, is the Hard Rock in Bali. It bills itself as the world's premier rock 'n' roll vacation destination and it has the bands and live events booked well in advance to prove it. This is certainly not an example of a new getaway that is offering its guests the chance to escape the hurly-burly of modern life and immerse themselves in the sound of birdsong and waves lazily lapping the shore. Far from it.

What the Hard Rock is offering, however, is the chance to tour the island on a Harley Davidson or to swim in a pool whose owners have been thoughtful enough even to pipe in underwater rock music. There is also the guarantee that your

every second will be occupied, perhaps with the hot bods and cool babes who are also part of the poolside scene that is featured in the online brochure. And should guests decide to retreat to their room for a while, they will find interactive video games there to ensure they do not grow bored.

This is lifestyle marketing at its most blatant, reaching out to the aspiring rock star in its guests and offering them the chance to indulge that fantasy in the exotic context of sun, sea and socializing with like-minded castaways.

Service included

Service is again an area in which the getaway hotel differs from other new hotels. In this case, the service needs to be discreet to the point of being subliminal, while managing to exert a more intensive and pampering influence than in any other kind of hotel environment. The aim is to excise any practical concerns from the minds of the guests while maintaining an atmosphere that is relaxed and uninhibited. This is usually achieved through a high staff-to-guest ratio – the Begawan Giri resort in Bali, for example, has a ratio as high as five to one.

Aman Resorts pioneered this approach with minute attention to detail and by second-guessing the needs of their guests. At the Amanpuri hotel in Phuket, for instance, staff delivered small white towels dipped in water and lemon juice to guests lying on the beach. In many ways this kind of service came to represent a significant turning point in the hotel industry. A new opportunity was emerging for people who no longer wanted organized Club Med-style holidays but wanted instead to operate to their own schedule while keeping the attendant perks of a five-star experience. In a sense, then, such changing consumer expectations and this kind of enlightened service philosophy together became a major driving force in the emergence of the new getaway hotel.

The new sanitoriums

The spa hotel dates back to the era of the grand hotel, when consumptive and frail members of the aristocracy would look to the cool, clean mountain air for the answers that medicine could not provide. But the new spa hotel is a completely different bag of salts. It is a logical extension of the pampering, cosseting service that is associated with the modern getaway, offering a service that has its origins in the demand for luxury treatments as opposed to any medical requirement. Ever more sophisticated spa facilities enable guests to make the transition to the ultimate level of indulgence in record-breaking time. What better way could there be to mark the beginning of a relaxing holiday than to book an in-room massage on arrival?

The preceding chapters have unearthed numerous examples of the symbiotic relationship between the new hotel and its clientele. It is a world in which change is instigated by shifts in the demands and lifestyle aspirations of the consumer. It is therefore logical that this more sophisticated customer base has prompted the modern breed of getaway hotels to develop facilities and services that cater for people who are looking for natural ways to soothe their frazzled nerves. The philosophy of healthy mind and healthy body – *mens sana in corpore sano* – is central to the lifestyle of most of the affluent customers of these kinds of luxury hotel assets. And they are looking for somewhere to recharge their batteries in style.

Inner sanctums

The range of treatments that is available in many contemporary spa hotels is also a reflection of the cosmopolitan mindset of their guests. One notable example of this is Chiva Som, a self-styled international health resort in Thailand. Accommodation is divided into pavilions that stretch along the Hua-Hin beach resort, providing the basis for what it describes as a controlled environment for its guests.

On arrival at Chiva Som guests receive a private consultation with a member of the hotel's in-house medical staff (encompassing doctors and nurses through to dieticians and other specialists). But the aim of the hotel is not to provide any kind of conventional healthcare; in fact, far from it. The literature states that the resort aims to care for off-peak rather than sick patients, treating them for ailments that are more inevitable side-effects of modern living – stress-related illnesses, skin problems, low immunity threshold and the like. Chiva Som is a prepackaged cure-all for the multitasked modern consumer, and it has the technology to prove it.

Alternative therapies

The spa facility is divided into a total of 21 treatment rooms and offers a wide range of massages, scrubs, wraps, reflexology, aromatherapy, and electrical face and body toning treatments. A separate hydrotherapy suite specializes in a high-tech touch, offering computerized massages. A jet shower room, a music therapy area and a state-of-the-art flotation chamber are the less physically rigorous remedies for stress. The resort also offers its guests the chance to have their massage out in the open air, surrounded by lush Thai vegetation and warm sunshine. Guest lecturers visit the facility and put forward the merits of their particular approach – perhaps a seminar on positive stress or pranayama yoga. Of course, the resort provides a healthy, balanced diet in its restaurant and even has its own cookbook for guests who are resolved to continue the good work at home.

The American-based chain of Golden Door spas invites guests to come and visit and just chill out, as opposed to offering the rather more highbrow medical approach of Chiva Som. The emphasis at Golden Door is on relaxation and pampering. Deborah Szekely modelled the brand on the Honjin inns of Japan, where travellers took time out from their journey to recuperate. The Boulder spa in Carefree, Arizona, is a perfect case in point. Guests check into the elemental Earth, Sun and Water treatment rooms for hot-rock massages or salt-glow body therapies. It is a sanctuary for the modern age.

The Hasseludden Yasuragi spa in the Stockholm archipelago has successfully planted its vision of the modern getaway resort in a particularly rugged stretch of the Swedish coastline. The environment is clean and minimal, entirely in keeping with the selection of Eastern-influenced treatments available to guests. Treatments vary widely, from

Opposite *At the Hacienda Katanchel in Mexico guests can enjoy a relaxing honey massage in idyllic surroundings.*

different kinds of shiatsu massage, tuina (a hybrid of acupressure, massage and chiropractic) and kyarabi and yasuragi body scrubs, to the more conventional facials and aroma therapy and energy massages.

Similarly, the Canoe Bay resort in Wisconsin has taken the architecture of Frank Lloyd Wright as the inspiration for its organically designed woodland setting. Massages are administered on the shores of a stunning lake and telephones are banned, as are children and pets. This is an attempt to reunite guests with Mother Nature worthy of Thoreau, and the operators have created a mini lifestyle to correspond with their aims. Carefully prepared country cooking makes the best of the region's ingredients, and activities such as canoeing, fishing and swimming in the lake are all heartily encouraged.

Perhaps the opposite end of the spectrum of spa destinations would be the Hope Springs in California, which has been designed as a funky getaway for the young that transforms city slickers into urbane slackers. Owners Mick Haggerty and Steve and Misako Samiof have given the mid-twentieth-century building set in the Coachella Valley a sassy makeover. Asian influences collide with cool modernism in the guestrooms and the arid poolside terrace is bristling with cacti and film-set Americana. The spa facilities have been designed for those who, weary after a day in the sun, are ready, for example, for a cooling facial before dinner.

Urban getaways

The concept of a getaway hotel need not be confined to the world's most exotic locations, of course. The luxury penthouse is a form of urban retreat that surpasses even the most discreet townhouse hotel. It is a mini palace for hire that is removed and secluded from everyday life. This type of accommodation is the preserve of the ultra-rich. Major-league expense-accounters and celebrities are lured not just by the space and extra amenities that

the penthouse promises but also by the idea that this is a part of the hotel that is set aside exclusively for them. It is a privileged destination shared by a select few, and the design must emphasize this fact through the use of luxury materials and the evocation of a discreet and refined hideaway.

The most striking example of this type of urban idyll is the triplex suite at the New York Palace in New York. Nestling high up in the Manhattan skyline, the suite boasts almost floor-to-ceiling windows that make the most of the skyscraper views. A team of French designers – Pierre Court, Jean-Pierre Vignaud, Eric Bass and Jean-François Pavier Salomon – has endowed the space with a sense of subdued elegance and understated luxury. The choice of materials is a crucial factor in the design, since it presents a prime opportunity to establish the quality and tone of the penthouse. Columns wrapped in black leather soar up to 5.5-metre (18-foot) ceilings and a swirling staircase joins the living room to the balcony. Furniture is simply upholstered, while rugs create bold blocks of colour. The overall effect is one that is intended as a complicit nod to the occupant, affirming that he or she is a part of a closed circle. In this case design is used as a tool for creating sufficient cachet and kudos in an interior that it can be marketed to and used by a discerning minority who are looking for a getaway hotel hiding in the heart of civilization.

Right The Tides, Miami, is the still centre of the spinning South Beach scene. Light floods into every hushed and whitewashed suite, and the existing 115 rooms were converted to 45 sumptuous spaces so that each would have an ocean view.

Opposite The Delano, Miami, is an oasis amid the bustle of South Beach. The palm-fringed pool area is called the Water Salon; also on offer are an orchid garden, a gym, the Agua spa and the macrobiotic Blue Door restaurant owned by Madonna.

new
arrivals

the standard

Los Angeles, United States

In the world of design hotels there is an emerging market that has little to do with five-star luxury experiences and pampering. The epicentre of this phenomenon is the buoyant and boisterous youth market, whose members' thirst for fun, cool and fresh new experiences has sparked some key developments in contemporary hotel design. It is a fast-moving scene, in an almost permanent state of flux, where the shelf-life of hotels can quickly expire as fashions and trends adapt to the pace of modern life. Even the accepted definition of 'youth market', for example, is changing. The term is now more often attached to ideas of type rather than to specific age groups, so the concept of young consumers tends to hang primarily on issues of lifestyle. Hotels targeting them find themselves wooing a clientele whose very fickleness is one of its defining characteristics and whose loyalties are liable to switch at the same rate as their allegiances to favourite nightclubs or bars.

An example of one such lifestyle issue would be the tendency among twenty- and thirtysomething customers of the new hotel to focus on pursuing a career, as opposed to settling down, getting married and bringing up a family at an early age. These days multitasked young professionals form a financially independent species of well-travelled, design-literate and confident consumers, with more available cash than earlier generations to indulge their passions. Lifestyle magazines such as *Wallpaper** may direct their hotel choice rather than the staid bibles of the mainstream traveller. A specialized breed of contemporary hotel has evolved to meet the needs of this niche clientele.

As its name suggests, the Standard on Sunset Boulevard in Los Angeles has established itself as one of the main banner-bearing hotels for a discerning elite of young travellers. Its raison d'être is to supply a stimulating environment that allows enough flexibility in the balance between formality and trendy chic to facilitate and even promote a lifestyle of urbane lounging. These are the factors that shaped the design. It is a witty mix of cool, crisp interiors and cinematic kitsch that has won the Standard a following among the media wannabees and about-to-bees. It is a far cry from its previous existence as a rundown retirement home when André Balazs purchased it. Before that it had been a motel.

The reception desk at the Standard is a particularly significant element of its design (see p. 67). As in all hotels, the reception is a guest's first point of contact both with the hotel staff and with the character and tone of the overall interior design, but Hausman has placed a greater than usual emphasis on this area in order to lay down his manifesto of youth marketing. The two defining characteristics of this space are the DJ based at the check-in desk and, behind that, an installation of performance art that consists of a girl reclining on a Barbarella-style bed in a tank set into the wall, like a huge, empty aquarium.

Opposite *Living up to its reputation as a hot destination hotel, the Standard has corridors lined with desert cacti and sand, and the wall tiles seem to have buckled in the heat.*

Above *Every guestroom has at the very least a balcony or a patio. The deep blue Astroturf of the pool deck, plus its pristine white sunloungers, table-tennis table and squares of mock lawn, extend the Standard experience into the open air.*

Right *The ultimate chairs in which to hang out and suspend disbelief.*

Above right *Bedrooms have a deceptive simplicity that is fiendishly hard to achieve – it requires the art that conceals art, and knowing when to stop.*

Far right *The guests Balazs has in mind are the kind who delight in entering a surreal world of trompe l'oeil deserts and flying fish.*

Within seconds of guests entering the hotel, the designer's cards are laid on the table. Hausman confronts guests from the very outset with the fact that this establishment is selling more than just a room for the night. It is, first and foremost, allowing customers to buy into a ready-made scene from the moment they check in. The design of the reception is an unequivocal statement, not so much about the hotel but about the audience it is seeking to attract: fashionable, certainly, but with enough humour to have fun. The hotel could be a bar, or a club – with a bed attached.

This statement is reiterated throughout the building. It resounds in the carpeted walls and ceiling of the conversation pit in the lobby, and reverberates around the red walls, windows, oversized pillows and squashy white sofas of the guestrooms. Each room has a silver bean-bag chair, Andy Warhol print curtains, an inflatable 'love chair' and an electric-orange tiled bathroom cleaned by chambermaids in bright pink uniforms, to clash with the colour scheme. All the ceilings look like chunky cottage cheese – a feature preserved from the days when the building was a retirement home.

This is the hotel of the future. Balazs himself says; 'The hotels I love are those that inspire excess in human behaviour.'

the townhouse

Miami, United States

I first visited Miami Beach by accident in 1986. At that time Ocean Drive was a rundown series of half-neglected hotels, where the state-subsidized elderly sat and gazed at the ocean, waiting to die. There was the News Café, a then revolutionary concept of selling coffee, newspapers and music all at the same time. The only three passable hotels, which went under the banner 'Art Deco Hotels', were the Cavalier, the Carlyle and the Cordozo; what shops there were sold artificial limbs, cheap wigs and spectacles.

Within a very few years the old people had gone, the hotels were all revamped in a garish mock-Deco pastiche, lacking any style (with one notable exception, Chris Blackwell's Century) and Ocean Drive was a traffic jam. Then in 1995 Ian Schrager opened the Delano and his and Phillipe Stark's design renewed demand for white nylon curtains, it being in perfect sync with Miami's youth-obsessed, body-conscious, lycra-clad revival.

Unfortunately, as large hotel operators realized the business potential of Miami Beach, some truly hideous hotels appeared. These were totally out of scale with the surrounding art-deco district and seemed to be attracting the conventions and crowds that had killed off Miami Beach first time around.

A number of stylish operators, though, have shown faith in the longevity of Miami Beach's ongoing revival, despite the fact that a few blocks in from Ocean Drive there are still areas that

Opposite *The Townhouse lobby is a conversation place. Guests who habitually resist being pigeonholed and rely on their mobile phones will happily curl up with retro telephones in holes in the wall.*

Above *Guests are encouraged to treat the whole hotel as their own vacation home. Every corner offers enticing spaces in which to flake out, read a magazine or finish a jigsaw.*

Above right *The rooftop deck is where guests can gather far from the crowd on Ocean Drive but still within sight of the sparkling waves. Identical parasols (but in white) grace the Tides a few blocks away.*

Far right *From seedy motel to edgy hotel, the building has had a miraculous makeover. Its snow-white exterior confirms for its target audience that this is the coolest place in town.*

seem to have benefited little from its new popularity. The W Hotel Group is opening a hotel, as is the glitzy Shore Club famed for its associations with Christy Turlington, Robert De Niro and Brian McNally (original operator of the Delano's Blue Door restaurant).

Jonathan Morr, who has established a number of successful ventures in New York (he has strong involvement with the hip eateries Republic and the SoHo bastion of Japanese cool Bond Street), put together a team of investors and snapped up a rundown motel on Collins Street just a stone's throw from the Shore Club. Morr's instinct is to give a much-needed injection of youth and frivolity to the increasingly serious hold on business here. To this end he gathered a team whose players have been involved in one way or another with the success of the Mercer and the Delano. He managed to bag ex-Christian Liaigre employee India Mahdavi and mixed the design ingredients up to create a cool hangout for the twenty-somethings who would choose the Standard as their West Coast home from home but were hitherto largely excluded from South Beach.

The concept is bright, young, and illogical, more MTV than MGM, but that is how Morr sees his market. The lobby is achingly hip, with circular niches half-lined with crescent-shaped cushions in poster red – the Townhouse's signature colour. Social and sexual intercourse are encouraged, washing machines are located in the lobby where hotel guests can meet the locals (should they feel in need of a tumble spin), and in the bedrooms the minibar stocks condoms in logoed packaging bearing the advice: 'Use for a good time at the

Townhouse.' If all this sounds like *Animal House* on the beach, Morr does not seem to mind. He points out that the revival of South Beach was due to the great climate, easy access and affordable accommodation; it was free of frills and was accessible to the young crowd.

The college kids and fun seekers do not have fancy decor or upscale restaurants on their list of priorities, because, as

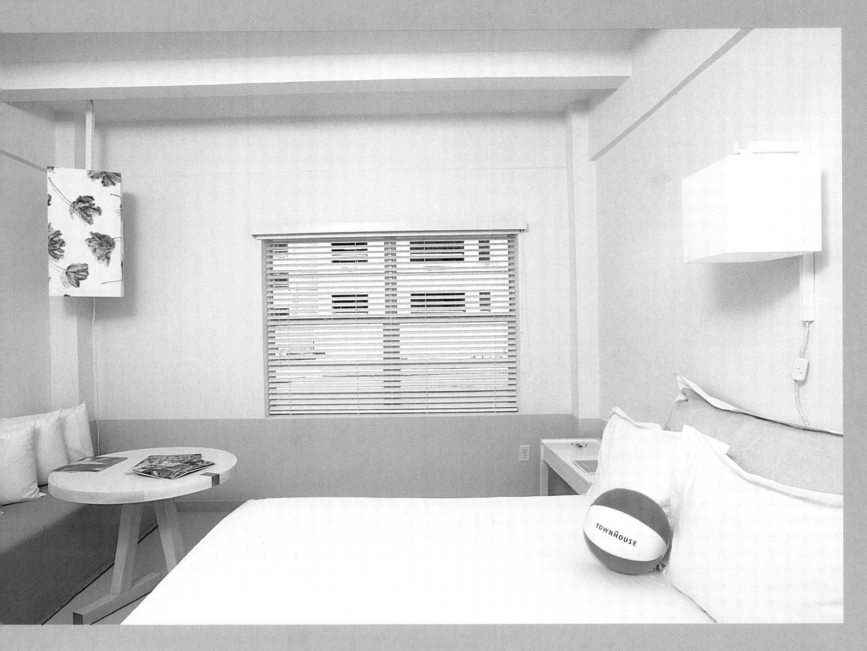

Morr points out, in Miami they are always at the beach experiencing its booming bar and club culture. They want somewhere simple and accessible where comfort means feeling free to hang out in the lobby or chill out on the swings in the porch.

The Townhouse does not have a pool and it is not on the beach – rather a disadvantage one might think – but it is amazing what a little lateral thinking can produce. Beginning with the idea that the pool scene is more important than the pool itself (who really wants to swim if there is a scene going on), the Townhouse boasts a converted watertower encased in glass where guests can shelter from the sun and cool off near the showers. At night the tower is illuminated to provide an ambient glow. Guests are encouraged to use and share waterbeds (you get to float on the water without the

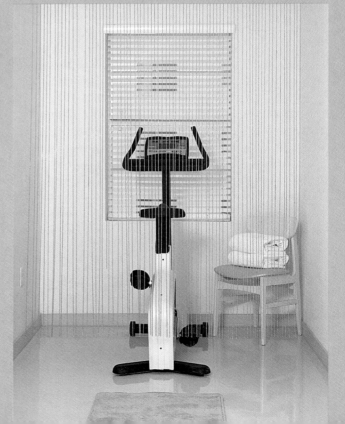

inconvenience of getting wet) and music is available through headphones. The hotel's press release gushes almost as much as the fountain: 'Townhouse is not a hotel... for one thing the roof is cool but there isn't a pool – you'll be mystified by the glow in the dark watertower while you float away on queen-sized waterbeds and swim in surround-sound stereo.'

Finally, should the thought of leaving these terminally cool surroundings prove too daunting for the Townhouse guest, they can try the Bond Street South outpost in the basement – a pared-down take on the eponymous New York bar. Guests at André Balazs's new, larger and bound-to-be-hipper Standard opening in downtown Los Angeles will also be able to try out its West-Coast equivalent, Bond Street West soon.

Above left and above *The bedrooms are simple, edited with the idea that the guest will be there for just a few hours a day. Key elements such as the Colgate-white bed and sofa and circular table 'on skis' are set off by rugs in beige, scarlet and baby blue. Morr seems to be more of a host than a hotelier. He has even provided simple L-shaped couches in the corner of the rooms where casual guests can 'crash' for the night. The rooms are given a quirky kitsch style with the addition of a dubious fifties-look floral fabric – designer Mahdavi's take on Starck's irreverence.*
Left *To compensate for the absence of a gym in fitness-obsessed South Beach, the designer has made use of the generously proportioned corridors to install exercise bikes.*

the hudson

New York, United States

Ever since the golden days of disco when he ruled over Manhattan's legendary Studio 54, Ian Schrager has been influenced by music and glamour. His hotels prior to the Hudson have indulged his sense of theatre coupled with Philippe Starck's lateral vision. The Hudson is the starting point of the 'chic but cheap' end of the hotel market.

This is the hotel as pop-and-rock venue, where the scale and exuberance of the public spaces are in adverse proportion to the carefully calibrated measurements of the guestrooms. In these minimal private spaces the guest is encouraged to do little more than rest, recuperate and refresh before going down to join the scene on the public floors of the hotel.

The Hudson is located in midtown New York, just a few blocks too far west to be in a really prime position, but then value of real estate is often determined by how much people want to be there. Judging by the constant crush outside the main entrance, Schrager and Starck have once again created a place where people want to be seen.

Always a canny operator with a keen sense of the 'next best thing', Shrager seems to have looked at the Standard in Los Angeles and quickly figured out that a market existed of increasingly moneyed college students as well as a growing graduate clientele. By tapping into this niche market with the affordable Hudson – the room rates opened at an astonishingly low $95 per night exclusive of taxes – he realized that he could net a new and upwardly mobile customer base that could in time be reeled in to his higher priced hotels.

Reminiscent of a university campus, the Hudson is a heady mixture of bars, pools, restaurants and fashionable shops. Few guests are likely to leave without having succumbed to the Hudson's invitation to spend and have a good time. Here the hotel is a living urban destination of shopping and sleeping.

Schrager and his team, headed by his business partner and chief designer Anda Andrei, have made ascending a full level from the street irresistible by transforming an ordinary escalator into a vision worthy of Alice's world through the looking glass. The 59th Street entrance appears to be fairly discreet until you notice the overpowering pulsating yellow chrome of the illuminated glass lobby that leads to the surreal moving staircase.

Scale is everything in this ironic take on fraternity house meets *Beauty and the Beast*. The lobby combines rich, dark wooden floors with an almost industrial backdrop of red brick.

Left *The restaurant resembles the canteen of an Ivy League college but, as ever, there are surreal touches to disorient and intrigue. Above the kitchen are giant images of heads silhouetted against leaping flames.*

Below and right *Since the aim of the Hudson is to provide value for money, brave short cuts have been made in the capsule-like guestrooms: most do not have ceiling lights and detailed finishes, instead there is exposed concrete and traditional wardrobes have given way to simple recesses with poles for hangers. Starck's sleight of hand, however, has ensured that the feeling is not cramped and utilitarian but 'friendly, cute and cosy'. Rich wood panelling and simple white furniture and bedding create in Starck's words, 'the interior of a little wooden egg'.*

Below right *Ingo Maurer's chandelier encapsulates Starck's belief in pairing extreme modernity with classicism: 'the tension and energy that this creates is very sexy'.*

The brick walls are finely pointed, and their soaring arches emphasize the building's vastness. The reception at first seems conventional, but its juxtaposition with the avant-garde Ingo Maurer chandeliers featuring hologram images of light bulbs, has the effect of a dream sequence from a David Lynch film.

Behind the reception desk and flanked on one side by the library and the restaurant is a striking and, for New York, a rare courtyard garden. In summer it is set out like a Moroccan pleasure garden with rugs, lanterns, candles and scattered cushions. The slightly unsettling presence of a three-metre high watering can sculpture is yet another ironic play on scale.

The restaurant is Starck's interpretation of a Harvard dining room with long wooden benches and communal tables that have never been so stylish as in this interior. The bar just off the lobby has shades of Stanley Kubrick. An organic, futurist tree-trunk bench designed by Jurgen Bey for Droog Design stands on an illuminated floor. Other furniture includes some of Starck's greatest hits from past projects plus newer pieces such as silicone Louis XVI chairs and vase-shaped stools, that seem to be levitating.

As usual the artworks indicate a keen understanding of fashionable tastes and a touch of irony. In the library, for instance, Jean-Baptiste Mondino's rather disturbing photographs of cows dressed in couture hats echoes an eighteenth-century vogue for dressing dogs as children. Everything in the Hudson is a play on usual perceptions and expectations, from the pool table that has purple, not green, baize, to the oversized Baroque armchairs. A declaration, says Schrager, of ' freedom and courage'.

myhotel

London, United Kingdom

myhotel in the genteel Bloomsbury quarter of London is one of the most prominent examples of the influence of feng shui on any modern hotel project. The hotel was designed by Conran & Partners, with the additional input of feng shui consultant William Spear. The aim of the project was to convert existing hotel premises into a contemporary hotel that incorporates the extra brief of an 'East meets West' design manifesto.

James Soane of Conran & Partners explains the fundamental thinking behind the interior design of myhotel: 'What we wanted to do was to make it feel like a domestic scale of operation rather than something grander than that. The idea was that by applying a contemporary design in what are essentially quite small rooms we could create the feeling of being a guest in a central London apartment; perhaps staying in someone's spare room. But there was the added consideration of the feng shui angle, which is something that the client was very keen that we should work into the design.'

The feng shui backbone of the hotel's design naturally necessitated some structural changes, such as the repositioning of the front door, which was deemed to be

Right *Beyond the street and pavement is a kind of private pavement with tables, followed by a series of connecting enfilade spaces connecting all the public parts of the building, finishing in the reception.*

Opposite *Both public and private spaces have been organised to allow positive chi energy to flow smoothly and positively, therefore stress-inducing straight lines, angular corners and sharp edges have been avoided, and soft, curvy shapes and warm colours have been used throughout to create a feeling of relaxation.*

inappropriately aligned and to be disrupting the energy flow of the building in its original position opposite the stairs. According to Soane, however, the most stimulating result of the feng shui input into the project was the opportunity to experiment with softer edges and forms within the framework of the interior design.

The reception and bar units on the ground floor of the hotel are good examples of these kind of distinctive curvaceous forms. The sensuous curve of the reception desk, which has a leather top and walnut cladding, establishes a kind of dialogue of forms with the equally rounded bar unit, which is differentiated by the fact that it is clad in sycamore and topped with zinc. There is a visual contact between the two shapes via a fish tank built into the fire wall separating the two spaces. Soane identifies the shape and configuration of these two features of the ground floor as 'very much a part of the feng shui brief, in the sense that the curve of the reception desk sweeps towards your body and that they are two rounded objects that are locked into a dialogue'.

On a more macro level, the design of the entire ground floor owes a great deal to feng shui principles. Beyond the main glass doors of the hotel, the public spaces – including the reception and bar – are linked by a series of enfilade doors, which are intended to reflect the idea of an 'internal street'. This was the biggest spatial move that Conran & Partners made in the lobby area and one that was designed to create an impression of a series of layers between the hotel and the street.

The basement library is another of the public areas that has a very deliberate design, in terms of its desired effect on the mood of the guests. Soane outlines how the design of the library coheres with the identity of the rest of the hotel: 'I think that the idea of giving guests somewhere that was a kind of haven fitted in with the philosophy of the hotel. The basement used to be a wine bar, with wallpapered brick columns, which was pretty unpleasant and so, in one sense, we were trying to create the opposite of that. We wanted it to seem a light and open space because the idea of an area that is a retreat or escape for guests could seem quite unpleasant in a way if it was underground.'

Irrespective of the actual implications of the feng shui design in terms of the energy and chi of the hotel, Soane feels that it was an important aspect of the collaboration between the design team and the client. 'The fact that the client so passionately believes in the principles of feng shui gave him great confidence in the project, which ensured the vision came to fruition'.

Top *The myhotel sign discreetly announces the establishment's modern, unpretentious aesthetic with a simple sans seriph typeface.*

Opposite and above *The guestrooms are the embodiment of elegant simplicity and have a strong Eastern flavour. Furniture was sourced from diverse areas: some came from Benchmark, other pieces were custom built for the hotel. In order to generate a difference in character and mood between the 64 rooms a colour scheme was introduced that evolves as you move up the building. The colours of the rooms, the furnishings and the bathroom tiling all vary according to their geographical location – North, South, East or West. For example, the northerly situation might have a bedside cabinet stained a clean white to symbolise the polar orientation.*

hotel de russie

Rome, Italy

The Hotel de Russie has an enviable location between two of the most charismatic squares in Europe, just a few steps to the north is the Piazza del Popolo, and an elegant stroll south along the fashionable via del Babuino brings one to the Piazza di Spagna.

The hotel itself is housed in a building with a vast amount of history behind it. Designed in 1816 by Guiseppe Valadir, it entertained a host of Russian dignitaries throughout the nineteenth century and from the 1890s on was the scene of grand receptions held by the Roman nobility. In the 1950s it experienced a radical restructuring by Count Vaselli. Its recent renovation has made the Russie a modern oasis of calm in the bustle that is Rome. Walking in off the street, visitors are welcomed by the restrained spaces and the long view to the back courtyard where they can discover a more sedate time and place.

The hotel was bought and rejuvenated by Sir Rocco Forte for his luxury hotel group R F Hotels and opened in April 2000. Sir Rocco's sister, Olga Polizzi (designer of Cardiff's state-of-the-art St David's hotel), collaborated with Roman architect Tommaso Ziffer to restyle the interior. Ziffer was responsible for the austere, restrained scheme that links the public rooms on the ground floor. He worked with a palette limited to diluted pastels in cream, mauve and beige in matt finishes, set against a limestone floor. The rooms are thinly furnished and have the appearance of tableaux rather than busy, thriving spaces. There is something in the furniture that imitates the current fashion for the work of the French designer Jean Michel Frank, who was renowned in the 1930s for his pared-down design, which does, however, demand only the most luxurious finishes.

There are 130 guestrooms in the hotel, including some 24 suites. All of the rooms are decorated in an international eclecticism of styles that is a novel treatment for a hotel in Rome, where most hotels in this category (such as the Eden and the Hassler) are determinedly Italian and Roman in their style. At the Hotel de Russie Ziffer has created a deliberately diffused collection of furniture inspired by Asia (the Japanese lacquer television and drinks cabinet) and 1940s Paris (the writing desk) as well as Rome (the Baroque headboard and acanthus-leaf curtain tie-backs). His aim was to achieve a contemporary look not by designing modern or innovative pieces of furniture but by adapting the international decorator strategy of assembling pieces from different areas and periods and arranging them in the rooms much as if they were treasures, gathered over a lifetime, in the apartment of a discerning globetrotter. Some of the rooms feature ebonized flooring which contrasts with the carpets set against pale pastel walls. The approach to the bathrooms varies, but whether classic or contemporary, a limited vocabulary of conventional bathroom materials (marble, mosaic, white porcelain) has been used to ensure that the bathroom style does not date.

To fit it for the twenty-first century and the fitness regimes of celebrity clients (Nicole Kidman, Leonardo Di Caprio and

Opposite *Designed by Valadier, the garden at the Hotel de Russie elicits gasps from the first-time visitor. From the back, it ascends through planted terraces to the edge of the Pincio, an ancient section of the great park of the Villa Borghese. This inspired use of a 'borrowed' landscape is brilliantly conceived, for there are few pleasures more beguiling in a busy city than a view of cascading greenery. Roman ruins and grottoes contribute to its romantic, fairytale charm, especially at twilight.*

Bruce Willis have all stayed here) the hotel now boasts a health club and spa with jacuzzi, Turkish steam bath, gym and beauty treatments. The best of modern Italian cooking is on offer in the restaurant and Stravinskij bar.

The design overall is certainly different from that of W Hotels or Ian Schrager, or even Anouska Hempel, who have done hotels in similar locations. The designers have respected the architecture and the history of the building and have tried to create an international style in a city that has one of the strongest personalities in the world. When time has allowed the hotel to settle into the rhythmn of Roman life we will see how it succeeds.

Left *The final touch to each guestroom is a photograph of flowers by American photographer Robert Mapplethorpe – an allusion to the so-called 'secret garden' of the hotel, perhaps.*
Below *An alfresco breakfast with a bird's eye view of the Piazza del Popolo – the essence of la dolce vita.*
Above right *Vaulted archways demand correspondingly splendid flowers.*
Right *Grey-suited staff at the reception desk convey a culture of formal, traditional service.*

blakes

Amsterdam, Holland

The designer and couturier Anouska Hempel created Blakes in London as the first designer hotel. It is chic, popular and still undeniably modern. This modernity comes from its ethos, which is to sustain a world where Hempel writes the rules and creates a total environment whose design, service and concept meld seamlessly together.

In 1997 Hempel opened Blakes in Amsterdam, on a site with a fascinating history. From 1617 to 1772 Keizersgracht 384, overlooking one of the three main canals in the heart of the city, was a celebrated theatre staging plays by Shakespeare, Molière and Voltaire as well as Dutch drama; and in 1737 Vivaldi conducted the orchestra there. Tragically, in 1772 the theatre burned down during a performance, with only the sandstone porch and hall (where guests now check in) surviving. The new building erected in its place was a charitable foundation for the city's poor; long rows of people would queue for food in the 'food stocks', now the lounge, and the former alms room houses a bar today.

The building remained largely unchanged for two centuries. When new owners acquired the property in 1998 it was destined for conversion to apartments, but the owners had long been fans of Blakes in London and approached Hempel with the idea of creating a Dutch version. On visiting the site, she was immediately captivated by the project. The layers of history, handcrafted beams, herringbone brick floors, classical sandstone porticoes and Dutch gables were irresistible. The result is a testament to the exquisite taste and style of a woman who in many ways designed a modern hotel long before Ian Schrager, Philippe Starck and Andrée Putman.

When the first Blakes opened, its exotic mixture of black walls, sisal flooring and Louis Vuitton vintage trunks was as unique as it was inventive, rebelling against the banal international look that was prevalent at the time. Hempel relied on imagination and determination rather than unlimited financial resources to compose a dramatic setting that has since attracted a devoted show-business clientele. It seemed inevitable that Blakes would be bought out and cloned – obvious outposts would be Los Angeles and New York – but, ever surprising, Hempel instead chose an unexpected location for her second Blakes. The laid-back city of Amsterdam is known more for its liberal attitudes to sex and drugs than its aspirations to offer stylish and individual hotels.

In this new hotel Hempel's palette was inspired by the history of Amsterdam, especially its rich trading heritage and close ties with the Dutch East Indies. The city's distinctive tall, narrow houses, so built because of the scarcity of land, also influenced her interpretation of Blakes in the Dutch idiom. The hotel contains 26 bedrooms, each of which was individually designed to arrive at the perfect blend of colour, texture and atmosphere. All look out on to the inner courtyard. One of the guestrooms was inspired by the spices sold by the Dutch East India Company; Hempel, who is poetic in her description of colours, likens the effect to 'ginger in a beautifully crafted slate

Opposite *The still courtyard is a sanctuary of 'silence and slow time', where evergreen oak and box grow quietly and a profusion of lavender, rosemary and other aromatic herbs scent the air.*

Opposite The restaurant is, aptly, located in the old bakery, which flourished from 1787 to 1811. The oven doors, lovingly preserved, are unusual and evocative period details. The food is a blend of the best of the classic and contemporary cuisines of East and West – Japanese and Thai with influences from Italy and France.

Right Hydrangea plants, which flourish in the wild in China and Japan, are combined with black lacquer in the Chinese Room.

Below Contemporary movable screens stand upon the carefully conserved original brick floor in the long gallery.

box with a thin layer of ground turmeric across the top'. Another is a quiet quartet of black, grey, navy and cream, suggested by an antique kimono. Rooms under the gables are white and beige, light and airy. Corridors echo the colour of the rooms they serve, imparting a satisfying unity.

Hempel understands service and the needs of today's luxury traveller better than anyone. Her minibars are stocked with canisters of oxygen, berocca, antistress vitamins, ginger chocolates, sleep masks, energy drinks and candles scented with amber and grapefruit. She says that it is 'my lifestyle that is offered here', and acknowledges that when faced with a choice between comfort and style, she will opt for style every time. Yet she undersells herself, for in fact she has the genius to make her designs so stylish that guests cannot help but feel comfortable with them.

The restaurant is an exercise in pared-down Dutch elegance. The black lacquer ceiling evokes the Orient and is a perfect foil for the original brick floor, which in turn beautifully

sets off the black and white colour scheme. It is Cecil Beaton meets Anouska Hempel in Amsterdam. Precise table settings match the geometry and order of the room itself. Lamps tipped with coolie-hat shades are lined up in a disciplined row like soldiers in the Chinese terracotta army, and furnish just the right degree of low-level ambient light. This is supplemented by theatrical spotlights set among the lacquered ceiling joists, which highlight splashes of green in the simple plant arrangements. Hempel's attention to detail also extended as far as designing the china in blue and white, recalling the Nanking Cargo, a Dutch shipment from China that was rescued from the seabed after quietly resting there for some 230 years.

Blakes Amsterdam works because even though it is the crystallization of one woman's vision, that vision is a bold one with clear parameters, an understanding of scale and impeccable taste. Designers seeking inspiration from Hempel's oeuvre have shamelessly tried to imitate her, but it has proved impossible to do so convincingly. For she is a one-off, and her brilliance flows in large part from her multifaceted background; she draws on her experience as actress, couturier, antiques dealer and landscape gardener when wearing the hats of designer and hotelier. She has demonstrated that her style comes from the pursuit of perfection, aided by her talent and sheer hard work.

claridges

London, United Kingdom

During the past few years the renewed interest in both design generally and the interior design of hotels has caused many of the established names in the hotel industry to re-examine how they look and perform in the brave new world of hotel design. Of course, all hotels are constantly engaged in renovation to a certain degree, from updating and maintenance of essential services to refurbishment of bedrooms. However, some of the most well-known hotels in the world have taken a giant step beyond such standard renovation. The Peninsula in Hong Kong, for example, is one of the most renewed hotels in Asia, having undergone a breathtaking reconstruction project during the 1990s that topped it with a new 30-storey tower. The rooftop Felix restaurant designed by Philippe Starck, with its unparalleled views of Hong Kong from the restaurant itself and the men's glass urinals provoked much quiet discussion among its old-school aficionados.

When Claridge's began upon its period of renovation in the mid-1990s the priority was to update the back-of-house areas and give a badly needed facelift to some of the upper floors and bedrooms. The conversion of previously private occupied penthouses proved a great success, customers judging that the resplendent suites merited the steep room rates.

The ground floor of Claridge's had always been a difficult area for the management to operate, and a confusing one for guests to navigate. It was a hotchpotch of different styles, some late nineteenth century but most early twentieth century. The so-called Winter Garden was the hub leading to the restaurant and adjacent to the awkwardly located concierge and reception desks.

A rarely used small restaurant with a dilapidated central buffet was the first area on the ground floor to undergo radical design surgery. Known as the Causerie, this had been a billiard room in Edwardian days, but was remodelled in 1920 by Basil Ionides in the English Art Déco style. This movement was not as widely adopted in England as it was known in neighbouring France. Many elements of its interior – in fact, of the whole of the ground floor – were Grade II listed as examples of architectural and interior design that should be preserved because of their historical significance and the rarity of any surviving rooms of this period.

Close consultation with English Heritage ensured that all of the room's notable architectural elements were retained, and key details sensitively restored. Within the parameters of scrupulous respect for the room's heritage, it was still possible

to change its configuration by opening up the long-blocked entrance from the street, reinstating the fireplace, re-siting the bar and creating a silk-upholstered snug in the previous service kitchen.

The resulting space, renamed the Claridge's Bar has proved a popular drinks destination for hotel guests (long deprived of their own bar) but also for the local business and residential community who have added life and atmosphere to a hotel that had been in danger of becoming staid.

The materials chosen are all in keeping with the room's heyday. Stripped of all its Art Déco finery back in the 1980s, it now features mock-crocodile banquettes and chairs, and a Venetian chandelier that was installed at the Grand Hotel in Rome in 1925. The parquet floor has a basketweave pattern and the sensuous black patent-leather bar is topped with an onyx counter.

When it came to revitalizing the lobby area, it was natural to continue the Art Déco theme. Though tackling his first hotel commission, Thierry Despont, the designer engaged, was no stranger to grand projects, having created the Decorative Arts Galleries of the John Paul Getty Museum and schemes for the houses of, among others, Bill Gates and Hubert de Givenchy. His guiding principle was 'to restore Claridge's for Claridge's... This is not about a designer redesigning Claridge's'.

The large space – originally where carriages deposited lords and ladies – now showcases Art Déco features by Basil Ionides and Oswald Milne. The carpet is an interpretation of a 1930s Marion Dorn design. In a spirit of *entente cordiale*.

Above left *Advice from English Heritage ensured the preservation of precious architectural details.*
Above right *Dale Chihuly's chandelier was fashioned from more than 800 handblown pieces of clear glass.*
Opposite *Some of the lobby's chairs are dressed in a striking geometric bouclé, an exact replica of a 1930s Betty Joel fabric. The carpet, in a Marion Dorn design, is the perfect partner.*

The brightly guilded new interior is furnished with copies of rugs and furniture by the 1930s designer Ruhlmann, overseen by a spectacular glass chandelier designed by Chihuly. Adjacent to the foyer is a new reading room with custom-made carpet, chairs and tables in Art Déco mood. Open fires crackle at either end and a row of columns glamorously clad in hand-stitched leather run down the centre of the room.

The lobby is now firmly set in the 1930s and so exudes a more fashion-conscious air. It also works better as a venue for light lunches and informal meetings. The concierge has been shrewdly moved to make the space function better. The dining room, which has been altered significantly over the years, now gets its own celebrity chef in the carefully restored interior.

mandarin oriental hyde park

London, United Kingdom

In the beginning there were the great spas/natural springs and the towns that grew up around them. The privileged were able to travel to 'take the waters in Bath', for example. In recent years, hotels have tried, with the ever-growing competitiveness of the market to incorporate the idea of the spa as an integral part of the luxury hotel experience.

There are many famous spas today; glossy magazines regularly compile their top 20. Some, like La Prairie in Switzerland, are strictly medical in approach. Others, like Chiva-Som in Huo Hin, Thailand, are designed for those who want to stretch out via daily classes of yoga and t'ai chi, lose weight with carefully balanced (mini) meals and relax during one of the many massage and beauty therapies on offer.

The Agua Spa was founded by Rita Schrager at the Delano in Miami, one of the first hotels to offer a designer spa. Judging from the success of the LVMH-operated Bliss spas, demand is clearly there for pampering therapies. The concept of the new urban spa – an oasis offering relaxing and revitalizing treatments in an accessible city location – is difficult to resist.

London's Mandarin Oriental Hyde Park hotel is located in the heart of Knightsbridge and was formerly known as the Hyde Park hotel. It changed hands after Granada obtained control from Forte. Since then, it has undergone a major programme of investment that has resulted in new rooms in the former staff area, and a series of new public rooms including a bar and two new restaurants all geared to updating the hotel's former image.

Its location, a couple of minutes from Harvey Nichols and the designer stores of Sloane Street, makes it easily accessible to the jaded shopper and the ladies who lunch. A number of new operators, including New York's Bliss, are on hand to cater to this ready-made market. At the Mandarin Oriental Hyde Park the spa is operated by the company E'SPA. Here the design and service are comparable to my favourite spa, at the Oriental in Bangkok. Undoubtedly, the spiritual home of the spa is the East, where relaxation and meditation are valued as essential antidotes to stress and tiredness. The concept of this E'SPA spa is to blend traditional therapies from East and West into a system of restorative 'rituals'. The visitor enters a calming reception area concealed behind a lacquer screen. Unusually, the advised arrival time is 40 minutes before the appointment, to give the visitor time to unwind in the relaxation areas.

The spa itself is approached through an illuminated floor-to-ceiling fringed curtain, and a softly illuminated staircase of rough-textured stone leads to the main pre-treatment areas. The client is encouraged to spend as much time as possible in these areas to benefit from the whole mood-enhancing experience. The special facilities include the sanarium (a gentler and soothing variation of the traditional sauna) and the vitality pool, finished in natural materials such as Zimbabwean granite, teak, pebbles and glass. Glimpses of daylight are afforded by showers looking on to miniature Oriental courtyards. Light, space and tranquility are the abiding sensations. Unfortunately, the basement location does not afford the welcome vistas that are associated with the East.

Opposite *Whereas the Delano's Agua spa is on the roof, the spa at Mandarin Oriental Hyde Park is a subterranean sanctuary.*

Left and below *Black lacquer, incense sticks, single orchids in minimal architectural containers and Japanese tatami mats of woven straw imbue the atmosphere with Zen serenity.*

Right and below right *Custom-designed beds by Azumi, candles and a decor of cream and dove grey lull the visitor into an exquisite limbo. A soothing foot massage to ease tired feet begins each treatment.*

The vitality pool, reminiscent of the black minimalist pool at Amanpuri in Thailand, contains hydrotherapy body jets as well as a carved reclining bench with jets that massage the entire body with mineral water. The steam room, with obscured glass walls, overlooks the vitality pool and glows with diffused light; within the room a large wall-mounted amethyst crystal is a source of 'positive energy'.

To relax the mind into a state in which the therapies can act with optimum results there is a Zen relaxation area complete with black walnut recliners designed by Azumi. In addition, calming music through headphones and specially prepared aromatic herbal infusions promote the unwinding process. All five senses are soothed prior to the treatments: there is the sound of Tibetan cymbals, the subtle scent of relaxing essential oils, colour therapy through mood-enhancing light effects in the relaxation room, the taste of herbal infusions, and touch in the textures of the wet area's floor finishes, the foot bath and the cotton towelling robes. Tension and fatigue fade away.

The colour palette is muted, with a celadon green used as the signature colour for the entrance. Other material accents are cocoa-coloured horsehair, crackle-finish lacquered walls, honed black slate, pale pebbles and wicker. Simple flower arrangements of orchids reinforce the Oriental theme.

The spa design succeeds in creating a microclimate within a busy hotel and the commitment to service helps the client to forget about the frantic activity of Knightsbridge just metres away from the hotel. The entire concept could, however, benefit from a slightly softer touch in the styling and finishes.

the medusa

Sydney, Australia

Australia is a must-see for anyone who is interested in new developments in lifestyle. Australian bar culture, restaurants and latterly hotels have a youthfulness and irreverence that allows them to take risks and succeed or fail but never be concerned about matters as prosaic as taste or external culture. Yet this does not mean that Australia displays bad taste and design – quite the opposite, in fact. With innovations such as its contemporary take on urban living and its fusion food incorporating Asiatic cuisine, it is now at the forefront of modern design. Magazines such as *Monument* and a string of stylish boutiques signal the enthusiasm with which Australians embrace new ideas.

It is significant that in Sydney international groups such as the W Group seem to miss their target market – today's young Australia has a strong sense of independence and seems to want to create its own style.

The Medusa hotel is set in Darlington, one of the oldest suburbs in Sydney, in an area that could be termed a cross between New York's SoHo and Paris's Marais. The Medusa opened early in 1998 to cater for today's modern traveller, and is the only hotel in Australia that allows pets (although you have

to sign a pet policy and a maximum of two dogs are permitted in each room). The man responsible for the design is Scott Weston, who, as so often in the homegrown contemporary hotels world, is an Australian. Weston's work at the Medusa completely deconstructs the normal preconception that a hotel interior should be designed as a calm, soothing oasis for frazzled travellers. He calls it a place of total seduction. His contrasting colour schemes, for which he is renowned, almost seem to leap out of the front door: the foyer of shocking pink and red, with its high ceiling and randomly placed sculpted pink oak leaves, is a vibrant and playful invitation to guests. But Weston has judiciously introduced the dark simplicity of the staircase that peels away towards the upper floors to provide a much-needed sense of balance and contrast. The reception area (again with a very high ceiling) is modern in its use of black 1970s-style seating, offering an airy yet formal environment that accommodates the honesty bar. There is no restaurant in the hotel, the reasoning being that there are so many restaurants in the area that another is unnecessary. However, the guestrooms do have fully equipped kitchenettes so that guests can prepare their own meals, if they wish.

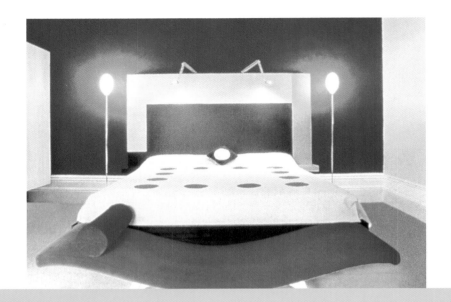

Left and below *The sinuous curves of the chaise, oval lamps and a cushion that squares the circle are Weston's way of working roundness into a strongly linear environment. The honeycomb circles of the balcony railings develop the thesis, in a creative interplay with the slats of the shutters.*
Far right *Bare white walls and intricate ironwork provide guests with the ideal conditions for meditation on a mandala.*

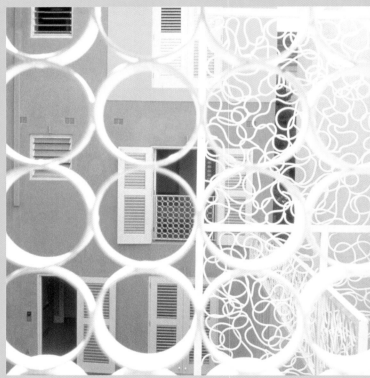

The guestrooms, which are mostly grouped around a bright courtyard with much of its original wrought-ironwork left intact, have received Weston's colour treatment. A clashing medley of blues, oranges and yellows bursts across the walls, floors and upholstery in each of the 18 rooms, so that the muted, pastel shades of the courtyard and the inward-facing façades of the building seem restful by contrast. The 'Grand Rooms' are very spacious, and although the furniture is essentially minimalist, they have a distinctly luxurious atmosphere. Mixes of timbers, paper chandeliers and unusual joinery create a slightly theatrical look. The windows are extremely large so as to let in the optimum amount of natural light. Modern light fittings next to the beds can be dimmed to produce yet another artful effect. No two rooms are the same, each taking on its own identity, yet all are stamped with the Medusa signature.

Weston has clearly decided to make a statement with his design; the graphic bedcovering set against a striking headboard, which contrasts with the wall colour, ensures that no disciple of Pawson minimalism will feel at home here. The rooms, which make such a virtue of pet friendliness, also provide a handy chaise – or psychiatrist's couch, whichever way you want to look at it. The bathrooms can be a little small, but this is because the building is listed and the architect could not make any structural changes. However, Weston has tried to make them seem luxurious by using a classic combination of marble and glass and adding touches of richesse with top-quality towels and toiletries. Although function and comfort had to be compromised because of the original architecture, most guests will feel that the sacrifice was worthwhile. Others, however, would prefer a less atmospheric purpose-built hotel.

Weston has cleverly woven the mythological symbolism of the hotel's name into various elements of the interior design: the serpentine water sculpture in the reflection pond, the carpet on the main staircase and the freezing gaze of the Caravaggio portrait of the Medusa herself, for instance. Thanks to the newly opened Palazzo Versace on the Gold Coast, the Medusa head that is so strongly associated with the Versace brand now defines two contemporary hotels on this continent.

The adoption of a strong signature feature and a vibrant colour scheme, as exemplified by the Medusa, entails a number of pitfalls for both the designer and the operators. There is a danger that the hotel will be known more for its cavalier approach to introducing kitsch decorating references in a Victorian listed house than for being a pleasant place to

stay, with a highly individual style. The decoration is definitely not going to appeal to everyone, and may in fact alienate some potential guests who use the web images to research the hotel before making a booking. However, the hotel is entirely of a piece with a suburb well known for its bohemian culture and eclectic mixes of old and new. With its intimacy and its location in a happening neighbourhood amid trendy cafés and restaurants, the hotel's owners clearly feel that it has a special appeal and that its confidence will be rewarded.

Since the owners also run the Kirketon Hotel in Sydney, they must believe that they have identified a product and a market that will ensure that Australia's days of colonization by international chains are over.

hotel habita

Mexico City, Mexico

Mexico has for some time seemed a dubious proposition for discerning travellers. The country's fluctuating economy, sometimes unpredictable political situation and resorts ruined by high-rise hotels have worked against its inherent natural beauty and stretches of unspoilt coastline. In recent years, though, a Four Seasons hotel has opened in Mexico City and the jet-set destinations of Costa Careyes and Las Alamandas (developed by Isabel Goldsmith) at San Patricio Melaque, Jalisco, are proof that Mexico has the clout to support luxury hotels. Currently, the most interesting new hotel is to be found in Polanco, an elegant district in the heart of Mexico City. Here, surrounded by designer stores is a chic boutique hotel in an arresting box of acid-etched glass – the Habita.

The monolithic structure – a cube whose outer skin is patterned by different opacities of glass cladding – was designed by architect Enrique Norton. Containing only 32 guestrooms and four junior suites, the Habita is happily bijou, its choice of quality over quantity signalling its aspiration to become a specific destination for the young well-heeled traveller seeking individual service and ambience in one of the world's most vibrant cities.

The Habita's design is relaxed and modern in a mix of styles – mid-twentieth century meets twenty-first. The ground-floor lobby, with its simple architectural lines and understated use of marble and mosaic, has an illuminated reception desk as its focal point. The ground floor also houses Aura, a contemporary destination restaurant. This is closely linked to the rest of the hotel by the long bar that acts as both a demarcation line and a connection to the lobby.

The decoration of Aura is simple and rather anodyne but the ambience is refined by attractive young staff, the music and the modern presentation of the food. While not outstanding on its own, the restaurant succeeds because of the attention the

Above left *The Habita's transparent exterior proclaims it to be indisputably a place to see and be seen in – the glass walls share the secrets of the interior with outsiders to a rare degree.*
Above right *The lobby's highly polished marble floor has its direct opposite in the rough, exposed concrete of the ceilings.*
Opposite *The necessary collection of room keys is made a design feature at the reception desk.*

Above *The rooftop spa is visually linked with the ground floor six storeys below by the abstract mosaic of black and white tiles, a copy – in reverse – of one by the lobby. Touches like these give the hotel design coherence.*

Opposite *The Area's generous fireplace – 3.5 metres (12 feet) long – ensures that even on winter nights the open-air space is warm and welcoming. Decking for the tabletops shows care in following through the design idea.*

designers have given to blending the architecture, the interior styling, and the bar area into a package with a strong and consistent image.

Since the size of the site precludes garden terraces, the architects decided to create an outdoor environment on the fifth and sixth floors of the hotel. The fifth floor consists of a landscaped decked area with comfortable loungers; glass is used here to form the wall of the gym, where guests can also indulge in saunas, the jacuzzi and massages. This is a micro spa, carefully planned to give the maximum amount of space. The diminutive pool works well, the decking extending to the water's edge, giving an impression of more space. The innovative design makes this a social as well as a health scene, in keeping with the theme of the rest of the hotel design. The fifth floor is linked via a simple spiral staircase to the sixth-floor bar known as Area. This is the indoor/outdoor space that works in conjunction with the Aura restaurant on the ground floor. The windowless open space affords breathtaking views over Mexico City, and to enhance its ambience at night there is a long fireplace that acts as a focal feature as well as a source of warmth.

The sleek guestrooms at the Habita are simple and monochromatic. As is always the case with such strict schemes the finishes and details are of paramount importance, and, in this case, they are well thought through. Eames chairs, finest white cotton and Sony Vega flat-screen computers evince a commitment to design classics. Air conditioning is efficient, wardrobes generous and the lighting is well executed; in each room a floating glass console is a clever solution to the obligatory desk, which so often seems like an afterthought. Bathrooms match the bedrooms with their white and pale grey colour scheme, although are less successful in terms of functionality – a case of innovative design not necessarily finding an improvement to more conventional solutions. The window treatment is highly original, allowing the hotel's façade to become a key element of the interior – the signature use of plain and etched glass defines the views in and out.

Above left *Bathrooms have a streamlined simplicity; the aesthetic is fresh and modern to appeal to a youthful clientele.*
Above right *Shades of white, cream and grey, combined with expanses of glass, imbue the bedrooms with an incredible lightness of being.*
Opposite *The brilliant clarity of the Mexican light is dazzling as it streams through glass walls and dances across thousands of white tiles outside the fifth-floor gym.*

dorint am gendarmenmarkt

Berlin, Germany

Berlin, one of Europe's great cities, has, because of its turbulent history, been slower than its counterparts in becoming a destination city. However, reunification in 1989 removed the obstacles that had made it a problematic place to visit. Berlin is now considered, like Amsterdam and Barcelona, an exciting European hotspot, combining shopping and nightlife with unique historical attractions.

As part of its current renaissance, billions have been invested in the area adjacent to the Brandenburg Gate, where hotels have sprung up everywhere. Unfortunately, many of these have proved uninspiring and could have been located in half a dozen other cities. The eccentrically named Four Seasons Karl Lagerfeld was one of the first hotels that had the courage to be German, a brave restoration of a former Royal Hunting Lodge.

In 1999 the Dorint chain decided to experiment with a small line of boutique hotels and chose the Gendarmenmarkt area, moments away from the Brandenburg Gate, for its Berlin venture. The site is an attractive landmark – a Jugendstil-accented building on Berlin's well-known 'Police Square'. Designers Klein and Haller were given a brief to create a total 'boutique' concept rather than an update of existing corporate style. This approach starts with the exterior; above the door a plaque discreetly signposts: 'Das Hotel Am Gendarmenmarkt', deliberately downplaying the Dorint branding.

The entrance is dramatic yet simple, then a glass walkway leads to a stone pedestal bearing a flamboyant floral display. The message is clear already – that the hotel is aiming to be contemporary and upscale. The designers have used pale but rich materials throughout the hotel so that the overall ambience is relaxed. Importantly, the use of marbles, black glass, leather and timber complement the historic building that houses them. The task of combining old and new has been achieved by means of columns and materials mixed with contemporary touches such as grid panels and streamlined Italian furniture. The scale of the ground floor was a particular challenge as soaring ceilings can often confer an impersonal atmosphere.

Throughout the hotel the work of two artists has been featured to great effect. Berlin artist/photographer Karl Blossfeldt (1865–1932) is honoured in numerous examples of his unique plant photographs, and a book of his photographs has been placed in every room. Blossfeld's study of the Saxifraga Wilkomniana, a plant that looks like an ice crystal, was chosen for the corporate logo, lending a strong sense of identity and history to the hotel. Huge abstract statements by another German artist, Peter Kockei, make a striking contrast.

The hotel offers two restaurants: the Aigner, a formal option housed in a classic room, and the well-designed Atrium Café, which successfully uses the vertical elements of a colonnade and horizontal intermediate columns to form an interesting geometric interior. Here the lighting is a key ingredient, giant yet gentle cream shades bathing the room in soft, diffused

Opposite *Berlin is buzzing again as in Weimar days, art, music, fashion and politics colliding and cross fertilizing to create a new zeitgeist for the new millennium. The Dorint am Gendarmenmarkt's public areas provide calm, reflective corners in which to assimilate the city's sights and sounds.*

Above *The discipline and decorum of two leather armchairs, symmetrical to a centimetre, counterbalances the drama and dynamism of an abstract painting by Peter Kockei.*

Above right *The stately stairway is strictly linear, but the curves of an urn and a chrome handrail hint at a willingness to bend the rules.*

Opposite *Black and white in a bedroom is the ultimate in urban sophistication, and marble says luxury in every language.*

light. The chairs are interpretations of a French 1940s style with dark wood and pale upholstery that mirrors the way the dark wood tables have been covered with white linen runners. The restaurant exudes a sense of luxury commonly associated with more formal restaurants, yet at the same time, there is an element of informality, which is appropriate for a room predominantly used for breakfasts and brunches. The choice of a monochromatic colour scheme works because the textures add warmth, as do the cocoa-coloured banquettes.

Thanks to the complex plan of the existing building there are a number of variations on the layouts and shapes of the 22 suites, 44 double and 26 single rooms. There are in fact 12 different bedroom categories in all. A typical room has an air of assured simplicity, with a pleated screen of white linen

acting like a wall or recessed headboard behind the beds, plain yet sumptuous white bedding, minimal bedside lights and a novel communication between the sleeping and bathing areas. This link is created by a mirror in the bathroom that can be adjusted to open a view into the room, the door acting as a screen to divide the two areas when it is fully opened. The wardrobes are upholstered, to provide textural interest, and underline the message of luxury.

This hotel is clearly aimed at the business traveller rather than the leisure traveller. The designers have included a well-laid-out fitness, or as they prefer to call it 'wellness', centre where energetic clients can work out beside large glass windows with panoramic views of the city. Those guests looking for less stressful activities can try the colour and music therapies on offer. These induce complete relaxation through stylish chaise longues, specially chosen tinted lighting and headphones providing a soothing musical escape.

The conference rooms have been treated with the same eye to detail, the showpiece being the Delphinium Room used for conferences or concerts (it has capacity for 120 people), which features a stunning illuminated, etched glass floor.

The Dorint am Gendarmenmarkt proves that by using materials and detailing carefully, thoughtful hotel designers can make a contemporary statement even in an historic building.

Above left The wellness centre caters for the hotel's predominantly business clientele, ever concerned with healthy figures. Televisions enable them to keep up to date with share-price movements.

Above Having crossed the threshold, guests are greeted by a flash of fiery colour against the cream of marble walls and floors. Bird of paradise flowers are a flight of fancy to refresh the spirits.

Opposite The cream and chocolate colour scheme is continued in the dining room. Comfortable padded chairs and banquettes mean the double-height space does not feel daunting.

the morrison

Dublin, Republic of Ireland

Dublin was once a provincial city living in the shadow of its past associations, afraid to compete with its international neighbours in the style stakes. Its literature, poetry, wit and music were world renowned but apart from boasting the best pubs on earth, it could not really compete in the stylish hotel market. A number of international hotel chains have had mixed results in trying to establish themselves in Dublin. The Four Seasons and the Conrad Hilton suffer from the bland stamp of the international format, whereas indigenous hotels have tried rather too hard to appear 'international'. In the 1990s the rock group U2, assisted by Grace Leo-Andrieu, established the Clarence, which was one of the first contemporary hotels in the city. This was followed by the Merrion and the Fitzwilliam. Yet the notion of a designer hotel that reflected the emerging cosmopolitan Irish society, an idea fuelled by the Celtic Tiger economy, was not fully developed until the opening of the Morrison in 1999.

With Dublin famed as a thriving social city where alcohol can lubricate the poetic spirit, it is only natural that the hotel's aim is to be welcoming and unintimidating. At the same time,

it has to create an image and style that are strong enough to hold its own in its busy riverfront location, which is not short of other drinking venues.

The design of the Morrison has a distinct Eastern influence in its materials, finishes and even its artworks. The synergy of the cross-cultural melange flows from the collaboration between Hong Kong-born, Irish-based fashion designer John Rocha and architects Douglas Wallace. The hotel has been a success from day one, a vital factor in its popularity being its bustling ground floor. Here the Morrison Bar has ample space and benefits from its own separate entrance. In fact one Dublin wag described the hotel as a great bar with some rooms upstairs.

Above *A mesmerizing carved wooden head is the focal point of the Lobo Bar, where the Zen concept of shibui, or disciplined strength, is expertly applied: to express the hotel's philosophy of East meets West.*
Opposite *A heart-stopping gold-leaf rising sun, designed by Brian McDonald, blazes above leather armchairs clad in red and white: the immanence is unmistakably Japan.*

Above *The Lobo Bar evokes the Orient with both traditional and modern touches. Ceramics in softly lit alcoves suggest the tokonoma of a Zen temple while a row of sleek black stools replicates a computer, symbol of Japan's Tiger economy.*

Left *The ground-floor café-bar is a tranquil area in which to peruse the Irish Times or engage in a challenging game of chess.*

Opposite *The hotel lobby has quiet corners in which to enjoy a coffee with friends. Clèa van der Grijn's effulgent paintings (120 in all) adorn walls throughout the hotel.*

The hotel is a conversion of three Georgian buildings so derelict that one façade was all that could be preserved. It stands opposite the Millennium Bridge, which leads to the lively Temple Bar area that has seen major investment recently, developing this area of eighteenth- and nineteenth-century streets into a hive of restaurants and bars. The Morrison therefore uses as much of its public space as possible to provide a range of drinking options. The principal entrance to the hotel ushers visitor and guest towards two large bar lounges and a restaurant, which they pass before arriving at the reception area. In so doing it has borrowed a trick from Las Vegas hotels such as the Venetian that make its customers walk through the casino areas in order to reach the lifts.

The features used throughout the hotel are dark stained woods, a neutral palette for the walls, large gilded artworks by Cléa van der Grijn and Waterford crystal designed by John

Rocha. The wedge-shaped corridors between the hotel's 95 guest bedrooms epitomize the almost spartan feel of the architecture as they melt away into their vanishing points. Since minimalist Zen schemes can be perceived as cold and austere, warmth and texture have been introduced through 1960s-influenced lampshades in woven wicker, rugs that are an updated take on the 1970s fleece rugs so beloved by *Wallpaper* magazine, and blushing velvet cushions and throws.

The hotel boasts a stunning restaurant: the split-level Halo Restaurant serves a blend of Irish and modern French cooking in an awesome atrium setting with a ceiling 100 feet above. The Lobo Bar in the basement is so-named because it is below the Halo – *lobo* is Gaelic for body. Following the Oriental theme, it offers guests late-night drinking in intriguing surroundings. The design is dramatic, initiating visitors into an experience far removed from those provided by nearby rival winebars.

Some critics have argued that the Morrison's design is too clearly influenced by other hotels, from the Hempel to the Mercer. The Halo Restaurant's asymetrical staircase, for example, is reminiscent of New York's Paramount hotel. Echoes of all these hotels are certainly present, but it is nevertheless a unique synthesis of East and West, and the epitome of all that is exciting about Dublin today. Above all, it has established a reputation for sophistication and comfort.

Above and opposite *Each room is a distillation of the traditional shoin Japanese house. Bed and furniture conform to the tenet of low-level living; the graphic simplicity of black and white recalls sliding lattice partitions; cuboid lamps echo paper lanterns; the vibrant green of exotic star fruit and the vermillion of a velvet throw supply the richness of a treasured kimono. Each element is a syllable within a perfectly composed design haiku.*

the lancaster

Paris, France

The hotel operator Grace Leo-Andrieu has challenged the fashion for modernism and theatrical indulgence within interior design. Born in Hong Kong and educated at Cornell in hotel management, Leo-Andrieu was given her first taste of top management by Warwick International Hotels, becoming vice-president of the group at only 26 years old. She followed this with more precocious achievements, going on to open eight hotels in the next five years. At the age of 31 she started her own consultancy in Paris, where she was given the opportunity to work on the Guanahani resort in the Caribbean.

Leo-Andrieu's first headline-grabbing design, however, came about through her collaboration with the French interior designer Christian Liaigre – they created the Montalembert hotel in Paris, which opened in 1990. It became a much-imitated hotel and has given rise to a small army of imitators, some, like the Mercer, in New York created by Liaigre himself. Others, however, which have used Liaigre's signature Wenge-wood furniture and pendant parchment lights have provoked allegations of plagiarism; in one case the Bel-Ami in Paris, on which Leo-Andrieu acted as consultant in 1999, incensed Liaigre so much that he threatened to take legal action.

In Leo-Andrieu's more recent projects, the Lancaster and the Royal Riviera (see pp. 200–203), her signature attention to the modern demands of comfort, luxury and understated elegance have been continued. This is combined with elements of classicism that satisfy her clients' preference for authenticity and a sense of history.

The Lancaster and the Royal Riviera nod to different but tangible classical influences. In the case of the Lancaster, its history as a townhouse built in 1889 for a Spanish nobleman and converted into a hotel in 1928 by a Swiss gentleman, Emile Wolf, enabled Leo-Andrieu to work with the glamorous provenance of every aspect of the building. She found a treasure trove of Louis XV and Louis XVI furniture, ormolu clocks and tapestries gathered by Wolf and his housekeeper in the late 1920s, as well as a unique collection of more than 80 paintings by Russian émigré Boris Pastoukhoff, who stayed in the hotel many times in the 1930s, paying his bills with his paintings. The Lancaster must be one of the few hotels that can boast of having had its own artist in residence. Many of Pastoukhoff's works still hang in the hotel today, illustrating his distinctive artistic style. Though famous for his portraits – his

painting of Marlene Dietrich can be seen in the Marlene Dietrich suite – he also painted some vibrant still lifes. Situated at 7 rue de Berri, just off the Champs Elysées, the Lancaster has kept its low-key entrance; in fact, at night, when the large carriage-green doors are closed, it can easily be missed. The hushed rooms on the ground floor consist of a magnificent drawing room and an elegant Petit Salon; both contain the eclectic mixture of furniture for which the hotel is renowned. The furniture has, however, recently been updated with some contemporary pieces by Christian Liaigre as well as the Paris-based company Modernature. The drawing room demonstrates an original take on the now rather hackneyed East-meets-West approach. Leo-Andrieu displays her knowledge and confidence in mixing both idioms with original Japanese lacquered nest tables, Chinese coffee tables and Jean-Michel Frank-inspired sofas, all placed on a subtly coloured checkerboard floor of stone and marble.

The fabrics in the hotel, many by Canovas, Rubelli and other European houses, are pale-lined and quiet. The Emile Wolf suite glows with gold and cinnamon hues; the Marlene Dietrich suite is decorated in the star's favourite lilac colour scheme, its style working within the clever interpretation of classicism for our times. Chinese watercolours are the signature pieces of the dining room and serve as a reminder to the visitor of the global influences on the overall design of this hotel.

The bedrooms in the Lancaster are faithful to the notion of Paris as the ultimate romantic destination. They are whimsical and echo times long vanished, yet at the same time they are low-key. In function they transcend their classic style to provide

supreme ease of living and comfort. The attention to detail ranges from the linens by Porthauld to the simplicity of the white bathrooms of Carrera marble with their washbasins carved from a single solid block, and exemplifies a contemporary artistry with classic materials.

The garden at the Lancaster nestles in the courtyard behind the hotel. It is accessed by guests through the Grand Salon and is overlooked by the dining room. As at the nearby Hotel Costes, the garden court is an integral part of the hotel. The Lancaster's approach, however, is more restrained than its fashion-pack neighbour's. At the Hotel Costes the courtyard is the hub, an outdoor catwalk to see and be seen at. The Lancaster garden, designed by Philippe Niez and Alexandra Schmidt, is a botanical delight filled with specimens from all five continents. Guests can breakfast and lunch in privacy on specially designed garden furniture to the plashing of an ascetic stone-and-bronze fountain that supplies the perfect sound effect, sublime and so fitting for the environment.

Above *Precisely placed pebbles and the fountain's mellifluous mantra give the courtyard garden a spirit of Zen tranquillity.*
Left *Some of the bathrooms were restored to recapture their 1920s splendour. An expanse of marble, an exquisite orchid, are enduring emblems of sophistication.*
Opposite *Screens of woven wicker in the garden provide private corners for intimate meals. A set of graceful garden pieces – tables, chairs and benches – was specially commissioned, made from iroko wood and engraved with the hotel's logo.*

the hotel royal riviera

Classicism is defined as a style, architecture or interior design influenced by the classic elements of Greek and Roman design. Over the centuries, there have been several movements that have reinterpreted, updated, and in some cases reproduced elements of the classic style. The fruits of these revivals have been drawn upon subsequently to enhance the heritage of certain buildings and their interiors. Grace Leo-Andrieu's Royal Riviera is a resplendent example.

Glorying in a stunning location on the tiny peninsula of Saint-Jean-Cap-Ferrat, the hotel presides over one of the coast's private beaches (reserved exclusively for hotel guests). It is set within two and a half acres of gardens and commands spectacular views of the Mediterranean; the mountains of the Côte d'Azur form a magnificent backdrop. Built in 1904, it shared its Belle Époque style with other opulent hotels dotted around this stretch of the French Riviera. Its recent makeover, though, is a homage to its two remarkable neighbours: the Ephrussi de Rothschild Foundation Villa and the Villa Kerylos. The former, built in the early twentieth century, was designed in the style of an Italian palace to house the exceptional collection of eighteenth-century furniture, sixteenth-century Flemish tapestries, porcelains and Impressionist paintings assembled by the Baroness de Rothschild. In 1934 she bequeathed it to the Institute of France. The latter, even more influential in the refurbishment of the Royal Riviera, was conceived and built at the beginning of the last century by the archaeologist and Hellenic scholar Théodore Reinach in collaboration with his architect Emmanuel Pontrémoli. Their dream was to create, on a site recalling the shores of the Aegean, an authentic Greek villa embodying all aspects of the Ancient Greek way of life as they imagined it. However, they supplemented their use of precious mosaics, Carrera and Sienna marbles, exotic woods, opal, ivory, bronze and plaster with the comforts of electricity, plumbing and the other benefits of modern life. The villa, in sleepy Beaulieu-sur-Mer, was donated to the Institute of France in 1928 and the museum offers visitors a rare opportunity to gaze at close quarters, upon priceless vases, frescoes, statuettes and other treasures of Greek antiquity.

The new scheme for the Royal Riviera reflects this aspiration to the ideal Greek civilization in its (almost too) faithful homage to the classic furniture, colours and details of the Villa Kerylos. Grace Leo-Andrieu has attracted accusations of pastiche and even plagiarism with this scheme but the museum's curators seem to accept the imitation as a sincere form of flattery.

After the grandeur of the hotel's façade, embellished with classical white plaster mouldings and balconies with filigree railings, the entrance of the Royal Riviera adopts the vocabulary of neoclassicism with aplomb. Classical elements include a marble floor inlaid with black and white tiles in two complementary checkerboard patterns. The palette is a sophisticated one of cream, pale olive, black and gold.

Opposite In the reception area typical crystal chandeliers were eschewed; simple bronze lanterns allude to the skilled metalwork of classical civilizations. The pendant lights introduce a historical counterpoint, having been inspired by nineteenth-century billiard-table lights.

The Grand Salon is an intriguing mixture of twentieth-century design classics with simple sofas and comfortable armchairs. The colours of spice and ochre reflect the all-pervasive influence of the Villa Kerylos (and are also reminiscent of some of Jean-Michel Frank's work in the Riviera during the 1930s). The architectural elements have been updated and simplified; even the Greek key pattern in the freize looks contemporary.

Proportion and harmony are fundamental to classicism, and the design of the 77 guestrooms and suites illustrates this as successfully as those in the Grand Salon and restaurant. Such now-expected modern appurtenances as minibar, television, safe and 24-hour room service are integrated into settings of classical grace. Pastel shades of peach, apricot and palest blue in fabrics and mouldings are soft brushstrokes of colour against white walls and cherrywood furniture. Marble bathrooms accommodate an imperial bathtub. In such a suite might F. Scott Fitzgerald have penned a chapter of *Tender is the Night*.

Above *The refurbished Grand Salon reveals Grace Leo-Andrieu's mastery of different design idioms. Noble columns, marble and Greek pictures bespeak timeless classicism, yet converse fluently with twentieth-century chairs and lamps. White orchids are a Leo-Andrieu trademark.*
Above left *The hotel's restaurant, Le Panorama, has an dining terrace for alfresco dinners on balmy summer evenings, while La Pergola, the poolside grill and bar, serves open-air lunches. Guests disinclined to amble to the private beach can lounge beside the heated freshwater swimming pool.*
Far left and left *The Bedford Bar has the cosy ambience of a British gentleman's club, holding a select gathering of up to 40 people. The black-and-white marbling of the gleaming counter is ingeniously echoed in the dark, grained wood beneath. Studded leather armchairs, some with geometric patterns, signal an insistence on superb craftsmanship.*

the hôtel

Lucerne, Switzerland

Switzerland is perceived by many as a conservative society, taking itself seriously – the 'Made in Switzerland' imprimatur is a benchmark for quality and reliability. Therefore it is surprising that the city of Lucerne, 50 minutes from Zurich and located in a beautiful lakeside setting, should have produced one of the most interesting examples of new hotel design in recent years. Of course, it helps that two talented and independent thinkers have collaborated on the project. The owner, Urs Karli, already had the more conventional Schiller and Astoria hotels in Lucern when he approached French architect Jean Nouvel about an avant-garde approach for his new hotel. Nouvel is well established, not just in France but internationally, and his Cartier Institute and L'Institut du Monde Arabe show that he is one of the most original architects working in the world today.

Nouvel's mandate was to transform a seven-storey Art Nouveau townhouse into a boutique hotel whose individuality of design, combined with a strong dining and bar experience, would help to counteract the fact that Lucerne is not known as a trendy or edgy destination.

The result is The Hôtel. Nouvel has created a building with a unique sense of theatre achieved by the use of dramatic, staged lighting that effects a play of light and shadow over the entire seven storeys; from the exterior, the windows at night seem like a film set.

Colour, light, darkness and shadow all play important parts in the design. The public spaces are open yet intimate, and the way light falls on the surfaces and materials highlights the different textures used. It is the range of materials employed that provides variety for the eye, rather than colour, which is introduced by the choreographed lighting. The hotel plays with contrast throughout. There are the simple, well-detailed public areas, where sight lines are integral to the design. The fusion restaurant, Bam Bou, is more extrovert, with its 'peep-hole' view of the kitchen, an instance of the recurrent theme that the hotel is an exercise in voyeurism. Enigmatically, we are never sure who is spying on whom – is it the public looking into the stage-lit bedrooms, or the guests observing the outside world as if in a cinema?

Whatever the subliminal message, it has succeeded in making the bar, known as The Lounge, a magnet for the local cool crowd, and Bam Bou has established an independent reputation for exciting French cuisine with Asian influences.

Top *The bathrooms are simple, some approached through a change of level and sliding translucent screens. Deluxe suites offer the bizarre yet pleasurable experience of showering in a bamboo jungle beside a Swiss lake.*

Above and above right *The Bam Bou restaurant is a feast for the eyes as well as the tastebuds. An ingenious use of mirrors brings the outside inside.*

Left *Nouvel's constant goal is to formulate a stylistic language distinct from modernism and post-modernism. At The Hôtel furniture and fixtures express this succinctly, as well as his maxim: 'leave nothing to chance'.*

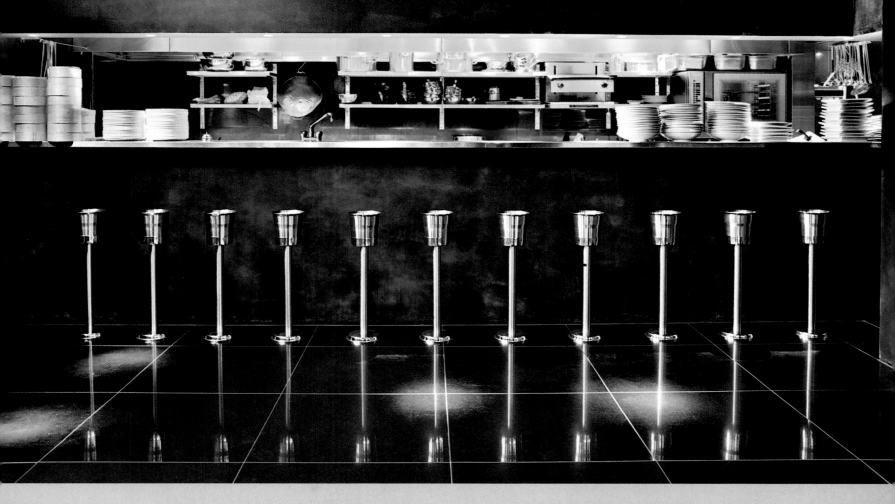

Karli believes that 'the hotel industry is entertainment' and this explains his delight with Nouvel's plans for the building: his concept 'was the perfect stage'. Indulging his passion for film and theatre, Nouvel composed set pieces within the hotel. 'Originally I wanted to be a painter', he has said, and his innate mastery of chiaroscuro is evident in the way he sets off his coloured statements against a dark backdrop. Corridors, which are plain black and featureless, throw into sharp focus the colours and daring theatricality of the guestrooms' design.

The guestrooms are well thought out, with recognizable Nouvel touches in the execution of the furniture. His skill in translating his vision from the architecture of the building through to the furniture is what sets him apart from many of his contemporaries, whose buildings are often compromised by the weakness and absence of vision in the choice of furnishings and finishes. What makes the design work so well is that the judicious choice of top-quality materials – the modest chair and footstool in the bedroom, upholstered in the finest leather – is more effective than the clutter of cheap furniture used by many hoteliers to furnish rooms.

The comfortable chairs, well-positioned desk and internet access are proof that guests at The Hôtel benefit from the perfectionist service aspirations of Swiss hotel operators as well as being treated to a unique filmic experience.

the chambers

In the late 1980s André Balazs tried to establish his first New York hotel, the Mercer. However, it took more than eight years of delays, abortive works and an economic slowdown in the early 1990s before the hotel finally found the right financing and partnership that resulted in its opening a year later in 1997. The key players were New York developers Ira Drukier and Richard Born, the two partners went on to participate in a number of other hotel developments including the Townhouse, Miami's take on Balazs's Standard and in spring 2001 the Chambers in New York.

The location of the Chambers – on West 56th Street – is a deliberate play to bring downtown style and attitude to the staid midtown scene, it is also a challenge to the celebrity favourite – the Four Seasons Hotel nearby on 57th Street. In reality, however, it is unlikely to provide serious competition to such an established venue. Unusually for New York, this is not a conversion or renovation of an existing building but instead an elegant, slightly European-looking townhouse erected on an asphalt parking lot; its 14 floors offer 77 bedrooms including ten suites. The large glass and timber doors are pointers to the strong design emphasis, which contrasts industrial downtown scale and finishes with a refined uptown layer of luxury evident, for instance, in alpaca-upholstered couches and cashmere throws on beds.

The designer, David Rockwell, has been responsible for some of the W hotels in the Starwood Group, and has brought with him some of the W's vocabulary – the clubby lobby, mezzanine space, two-storey feature fireplace – but in a rather cramped space. The result is a sort of down-scale W hotel.

This emphasis on the exhilarating collection of contemporary art (there are more than 500 works by of-the-moment artists and sculptors) is a key element in the design. Just as the VIP rooms in the Palladium used artists such as Kenny Schart to personalise their décor, each of the corridors at the Chambers was assigned to an artist to decorate.

The lobby adopts a common approach used in boutique hotels, fostering the illusion of having stepped into someone's home; it aspires to resemble the home of a wealthy collector with an eclectic taste for art and an eye for creating intimate seating areas. The owners and designer looked for inspiration to the nearby fashion stores (Gucci, Prada et al) to see how their target market wants to live. The resultant colours are fashionably muted, with texture a key factor in differentiating various areas and tones.

At the rear of the hotel is the almost mandatory in-house restaurant with a well-known chef. In this case the restaurant – Town – is the brainchild of chef Geoffrey Zakarian, formerly associated with restaurants Patroon and 44 at the Royalton. It is aimed at the fashionable crowd from midtown, with an emphasis on creating a space where, just like the hotel itself, the previously polarized uptown/downtown New York worlds can meld together.

Opposite Drukier's concept was to create a 'living museum' that would showcase art by an international selection of cutting-edge talents. Like the hotel design, the works are clever, witty and thought-provoking, aperitifs for the feast at the MOMA near by.

The design of the bedrooms is reminiscent of SoHo artists' lofts but with a more industrial take on them compared to the elegant minimalist look of the Mercer's bedrooms. The ceilings are supposed to be loft-like, but unfortunately they are not high enough to disguise the unfinished concrete, which looks unfinished cheap, as opposed to industrial chic. Even though the service pipes are exposed on the ceiling and the bedside lamps are (to put it kindly) utilitarian, they are counterbalanced by costly bedlinen by Archipelago and luxurious leather-upholstered wardrobes.

The scale of the furniture and furnishings make the rooms seem over-furnished with no space to move. The bed and the well-stocked media unit are considerably lower than is usual. This downplaying of the bed as the major design statement and focal point of the room is a significant move away from the trend introduced by Starck at the Royalton and widely followed. Rockwell touches include desks constructed from two wooden trestles topped with a sheet of glass bearing rolls of paper printed with maps of Manhattan, to be torn off and taken out by guests new to the city.

The bathrooms have an innovative, if impractical, feature of placing the basin outside with very little lighting and not much more storage. The concrete floor in the bathroom seems cold, and where it joins the adjustable shower, it provides a challenge to the unwary. Although the bathroom has more than its share of lights, it remains to be seen if the uptown crowd will come round to this style.

Opposite *Each guestroom has a minimum of five original artworks, which supply colour and drama in the otherwise restrained scheme. The furniture is mainly of grey-washed oak, with a stylish twist in terms of hand-rubbed blackened steel. In the Chambers, as in the Mercer, the careful editing of an eclectic assortment of furniture realizes the owners' vision of each room seeming personalized.*

Above left *The hotel's 14 storeys were each allocated to one of the 100 artists represented, so the corridors look strikingly different. Decorative methods include frescos, silk-screened wallpaper, photography and mixed media. Doors of mellow wood are plain, so as not to compete.*

Above right *Lavish leather tiles line the elevators. At least one wall is entirely glass, revealing the shaft and mechanics.*

conclusion

From the earliest inns to the latest arrivals,

we have travelled through the history of the hotel and observed its development

from offering basic bed and board to providing the most sophisticated blend of

technology and esoteric services. The core function of the hotel has not really

changed: what has altered is the way we live and how we want to spend our

time, and this has affected how we expect hotels to fulfil our requirements.

We are constantly evolving in our attitudes to work and leisure. Ideally, we

want more free time to indulge ourselves when we are not working, yet email,

modems and mobile palmtops ensure that around-the-clock business is

inescapable. We want to relax with our family and yet retain our independence;

we want to travel to exotic destinations and be sure of the climate when we get

there – guaranteed snow or sun depending on where we are going. It is clear

from all these contradictions that hotels can never offer everything to everyone,

since each person has a different idea of what is essential. In order to capture

their share of business, hotels have to be as flexible and sophisticated or

conversely as reliable and predictable as their clients.

As the world's climate changes, by what are now perceptible degrees, there

will be a noticeable impact on the entire hotel industry. The domino effect of

problems with holidays blighted by uncertain weather, and with other businesses

dependent on travel, will take its toll on hotels worldwide. Those hotels that are based on the concepts now being developed by expansion-hungry conglomerates or the optimistic single operator will have to be more aware than ever of exactly what their place in the market should be.

As you will have seen from the preceding chapters, particularly the one focusing on new arrivals, experimental design is not always a desirable ingredient in the recipe for success. Some of the so-called design hotels are trying so hard to make a statement that in the end they fail in their objective to create a well-thought-out, functional yet stimulating space for their guests.

At one time the vogue for traditional English style was so prevalent that from London to Hong Kong there was a universal interpretation of English tradition, characterized by patterned carpets, curtains and upholstery. This style gave way to the watered-down 'East meets West' syndrome in which it was thought that Zen and the secrets of Eastern calm and wellbeing could be obtained by lining up a row of potted orchids and installing wooden blinds. At the moment, pared-down minimalism fights with quirky 'ironic' design where kitsch is seen to be the new good taste. All of these styles have their merits and they should be judged not on how they conform to an individual taste but rather on how they perform in terms of quality, context, detailing and function.

The allure of hotels that have remembered to attach great importance to these crucial elements will not fade. While renewal and upgrading is always part of a hotel's natural lifecycle, ensuring that careful thought and planning informs every phase – from the early stages of design right through to the actual implementation – will avoid the style becoming obsolete and dated.

I see the future role of hotels becoming increasingly challenging. We want to travel further and further and yet at the same time spend less time getting there. We are able to access almost any spot on the globe within 24 hours and there are fewer and fewer truly obscure destinations. This means that hotels must meet all their customers' aspirations to the highest standard – from the spa to the signature restaurant – and at the same time remain ever aware of the need to keep ahead of the competition.

The urban hotel and the business-orientated hotel need to offer the kind of environment that will at the very least match our homes in comfort and style. Consumer spending on the home and associated fields including travel lifestyle products now exceeds the total spend on fashion and clothing in many markets. A significant future trend will show more fashion houses moving into the branded-hotel business; examples of those already involved include Versace's Palazzo Versace on the Gold Coast in Australia, Ferragamo's Gallery Hotel Art in Florence and Diesel's Pelican in Miami.

At the end of the day, the success of new hotel design will be judged by its longevity as much as by any other criteria. Designers will face a constant challenge to create something that is both new and timeless.

list of hotels

Adelphi
187 Flinders Lane, Melbourne, Victoria
  3000, Australia
tel +61 3 9650 7555
fax +61 3 9650 2710

Amanpuri
Pansea Beach, Phuket 83000, Thailand
tel +66 76 324 333
fax +66 76 324 100

Atelier sul Mare
Via Cesare Battisti 4, Castel di Tusa,
  Messina, Sicily, Italy
tel +39 0921 334295
fax +39 0921 334283

XV Beacon
15 Beacon St, Boston, MA 02108, USA
tel +1 617 670 1500
fax +1 617 670 2525

Begawan Giri
PO Box 54, Ubud, Bali 80571, Indonesia
tel +62 361 978888
fax +62 361 421872

Belaggio
33600 Las Vegas Boulevard South, Las
  Vegas, NV 89177, USA
tel +1 702 693 7111
fax +1 702 693 8546

Blakes, Amsterdam
Keizersgracht 384, 1016 GB, Amsterdam,
  Netherlands
tel +31 20 530 2010
fax +31 20 530 2030

Blakes, London
33 Roland Gardens, London SW7 3PF, UK
tel +44 171 370 6701
fax +44 171 373 0442

Hotel Bora Bora
Point Railtiti B.P.I, Bora Bora,
  French Polynesia
tel +689 604 411
fax +689 604 422

Chambers
15 West 56 St, New York, NY 10019, USA
tel +1 212 974 5656
fax +1 212 974 5657

Chiva Som
73/4 Petchkasem Road, Hua Hin 77110,
  Thailand
tel +66 32 536 536
fax +66 32 511 154

Claridge's
Brook St, Mayfair, London, W1A 2JQ, UK
tel +44 20 7629 8860
fax +44 20 7499 2210

Compass Point
PO Box CB-13842, West Bay St, Gambier,
  Nassau, The Bahamas
tel +1 242 327 4500
fax +1 242 327 2398

Hôtel Costes
239 rue St-Honoré, 75001 Paris, France
tel +33 1 4244 5000
fax +33 1 4244 5001

Delano
1685 Collins Avenue, Miami Beach, Florida
  33139, USA
tel +1 305 672 2000
fax +1 305 532 0099

Devigarh Palace
Delwara Nathdwara, Rajsamand, Udaipur,
  RA 31 3001, India
tel +91 2953 89211 20
fax +91 2953 89357

Dorint Am Gendarmenmarkt
Charlottenstraße 50–52, 10117 Berlin -
  Mitte Germany
tel +49 302 03 75 0
fax +49 302 03 75 100

Four Seasons
57 East 57th St, New York, NY 10022, USA
tel +1 212 758 57 00
fax +1 212 758 57 11

Hotel Habita
Av Presidente Masaryk 201, Col Polanco,
  Mexico
tel +52 5282 3100
fax +52 5282 3101

Hard Rock Hotel (Bali)
Jalan Pantai, Banjar Pande Mas, Kuta, Bali,
  Indonesia
tel +62 361 761 869
fax +62 361 761 868

Hard Rock Hotel (Las Vegas)
4455 Paradise Rd, Las Vegas, NV 89109,
  USA
tel +1 702 693 5000
fax +1 702 693 5014

Hempel
31–35 Craven Hill Gardens, London W2, UK
tel +44 20 7298 9000
fax +44 20 7402 4666

L'Hôtel

13 rue des Beaux-Arts, 75006 Paris, France

tel +33 1 4441 9900

fax +33 1 4325 6481

The Hotel

Sempacherstrasse 14, CH-6002 Lucerne,
  Switzerland

tel +41 41 226 86 86

fax +41 41 226 86 90

Hudson

356 West 58 St, New York, NY 10019, USA

tel +1 212 554 6000

fax +1 212 554 6001

Ice Hotel

Marknadsvägen 63, S-981 91 Jukkasjärvi,
  Sweden

tel +46 0980 668 00

fax +46 0980 668 90

Kirketon

229 Darlinghurst Road, Darlinghurst, Sydney
  2010 NSW, Australia.

tel +61 2 9332 2011

fax +61 2 9332 2499

Hôtel Lancaster

7, Rue de Berri, Champs Elysées, 75008
  Paris, France

tel +33 1 40 76 40 76

fax +33 1 40 76 40 10

Lygon Arms

Broadway, Worcestershire, WR12 7DU, UK

tel +44 1386 852255

fax +44 1386 858611

Mandarin Oriental Hyde Park

66 Knightbridge, London, SW1X 7LA, UK

tel +44 7235 2000

fax +44 7235 4552

Medusa

267 Darlinghurst Road, Darlinghurst,
  Sydney, 2010 NSW, Australia

tel +61 2 9331 1000

fax +61 2 9380 6901

Mercer

147 Mercer St, New York, NY 10012, USA

tel +1 212 966 6060

fax +1 212 965 3838

The Metropolitan

Old Park Lane, London, W1Y 4LB, UK

tel +44 20 7447 1000

fax +44 20 7447 1100

The Morrison Hotel

Ormond Quay, Dublin, Republic of Ireland

tel +353 1 887 2400

fax +353 1 878 3185

Myhotel

11–13 Bayley St, Bedford Squre, London,
  WC1 B 3HD, UK

tel +44 20 7667 6000

fax +44 20 7667 6044

One Aldwych

London, WC2B 4RH, UK

tel +44 20 7300 1000

fax +44 20 7300 1001

Pink Sands Resort

Harbour Island, Bahamas

tel +242 333-2030

fax +242 333-2060

Pousada Santa Maria de Flor da Rosa

7430 Crato, Portugal

tel +351 245 997 210

fax +351 245 997 212

Prince of Wales

2B Acland St, St Kilda, Melbourne, Australia

tel +61 3 9536 1111

fax +61 3 9536 1183

Regent Wall St

55 Wall St, New York, NY 10005, USA

tel +212 845-8600

fax +212 845-8601

Royal Riviera – St-Jean-Cap-Ferrat

3 Avenue Jean Monnet, 06230 Saint-Jean-
  Cap-Ferrat, France

tel +33 04 9376 3100

fax +33 04 9301 2307

Hôtel de Russie

Via del Babuino, 9 00187 Roma, Italy

tel +39 0632 8881

fax +39 0632 8888 88

Saint Martins Lane Hotel

45 St. Martins Lane, London, WC2N 4HX

tel +44 20 7300 5500

fax +44 20 7300 5501

Sanderson

50 Berners St, London WlP 3AD, UK

tel +44 20 7300 9500

fax +44 20 7300 1401

SoHo Grand

310 West Broadway at Grand St, New York,
  NY 10013, USA

tel +1 212 965 3000

fax +1 212 965 3200

The Standard

8300 Sunset Blvd., West Hollywood, CA
  90069, USA

tel +1 323 650 9090

fax +1 323 650 2820

Strawberry Hill

Irish Town P.A., St Andrew, Jamaica
  Goldeneye, Jamaica

tel +876 944 8400

fax +876 944 8408

Townhouse

150 20th St, Miami Beach, FL 33139, USA

tel +1 305 534 3800

fax +1 305 534 3811

TriBeCa Grand

310 West Broadway, Two Avenue of the
  Americas, New York, NY 10013, USA

tel +1 212 519 6600

fax +1 212 519 6700

Villa d'Este, Lake Como

22012 Cernobbio, Lago di Como, Italy

tel +39 0313 481

fax +39 0313 488 44

Hotel im Wasserturm

Kaygasse 2, 50676 Cologne, Germany

tel +49 221 200 80

fax +49 221 200 88 88

index

acknowledgements

Conran Octopus would like to thank the following photographers and organisations for their permission to reproduce the photographs in this book:

2–3 Axiom Photographic Agency/James Morris; 4–5 Axiom Photographic Agency/James Morris; 5 inset left Axiom Photographic Agency/James Morris; 5 inset centre & right Tim Street-Porter; 6 Andreas von Einsiedel.

Introduction
9 Angelo Hornak; 10 Travel Ink/Ronald Badkin; 11 Ray Main/Mainstream; 12 Fernando Bengoechea; 13 Condé Nast Publications Ltd/© *Condé Nast Traveller*/Simon Wheeler; 14–15 Christian Sarramon; 16 above The Interior Archive/Simon Upton; 16 below Ricardo Labougle.

Architectural Approaches
19 The Interior Archive/Simon Upton; 20 Agence Top/Pierre Hussenot; 21 Villa d'Este; 22–23 *World of Interiors*/Peter Grant; 24 Christian Sarramon; 25 German del Sol; 26 Duccio Malagamba/architect Eduardo Souto de Moura ; 27 The Interior Archive/Ken Haydn; 28 Hotel Gastwerk; 29 Nancy J Friedman PR; 30 The Prince Hotel/Earl Carter; 32 Hotel Pelirocco; 33 Lanny Provo; 35 Ray Main/Mainstream

Signage and Branding
37 Undine Pröhl; 39 People's Revolution PR/Grey Crawford ; 40 above left Blakes Hotel; 40 below left The Interior Archive/Fritz von der Schulenburg; 40 below right Burley Katon Halliday; 42 The Interior Archive/*House & Leisure*/Jac de Villiers; 43 Axiom Photographic Agency/James Morris; 44 Camera Press/Ilpo Musto; 46–47 The Interior Archive/Fritz von der Schulenburg; 48–49 Lynn Donaldson; 50 above left Les Publications Condé Nast S.A./© *Architectural Digest*, France/Vincent Knapp; 50 above right Das Hotel am Gendarmenmarkt; 50 below right Deidi von Schaewen;

Making an Entrance
53 Dan Klores Associates; 54 One Aldwych; 55 Purple PR/Todd Eberle; 56 Ricardo Labougle; 58 left Purple PR/Todd Eberle; 58 right *Marie Claire Maison*/Eric Morin/Daniel Rozensztroch; 59 Purple PR/Todd Eberle; 60 Bellagio Hotel; 61 Deidi von Schaewen; 62 Condé Nast Publications Ltd/© *Condé Nast Traveller*/Simon Wheeler; 63 José King; 64 Simon Kenny; 65 The Time Hotel; 66 Camera Press/Michael Franke/*Time Out*; 67 Tim Street-Porter.

Elements of Style
69 Richard Davies; 71 Michael Mundy; 72 The Time Hotel; 73 Agence Top/Xavier Desmier/decoration Jacques Garcia; 74

Simon Watson; 75 left Dan Klores Associates; 75 right Nancy J Friedman PR (designer Calvin Tsao); 76 left Simon Watson; 76 right The Prince Hotel/Earl Carter; 77 Christoph Kicherer; 79 Tim Street-Porter; 80 Axiom Photographic Agency/James Morris/(The Hempel, chairs designed by Mark Newson); 81 Richard Davies; 82–83 Trevor Mein; 85 above left Deidi von Schaewen/architect Christian Dorner; 85 below left Lanny Provo; 85 right Duccio Malagamba/architect Eduardo Souto de Moura; 86 Preston-Schlebusch; 87 Richard Davies; 88 Simon Watson; 89 left James Merrell; 89 right Ray Main/Mainstream.

Room Service
91 Fernando Bengoechea; 93 Preston-Schlebusch; 94 Ray Main/Mainstream; 95 The Interior Archive/Andrew Wood/designer Anouska Hempel; 96 left The Interior Archive/Simon Upton; 96 right The Ace Hotel/Matthew Kern; 97 Nancy J Friedman PR; 98–99 The Prince Hotel/Earl Carter; 101 left Deidi von Schaewen; 101 right Nancy J Friedman PR.

The Urban Hotel
103 Andreas von Einsiedel; 104 Helen Fickling;105 Condé Nast Publications Ltd/© *Vogue Entertaining & Travel*/Geoff Lung;106 David Collins/Andrew Lamb; 107 Arcaid/Piers Paiba; 108 Simon Watson; 109

Christian Sarramon; 110 Trevor Mein; 111 Condé Nast Publications Ltd/© *Condé Nast Traveller*/David Loftus; 112 Christoph Kicherer; 113 Morley von Sternberg; 114 Les Publications Condé Nast S.A./ © *Architectural Digest*, France/Noelle Hoeppe.

The Getaway Hotel

117 Preston-Schlebusch; 118–119 Deidi von Schaewen; 120 *World of Interiors*/Alex Ramsay; 121 Deidi von Schaewen; 122 Columbus Communications Island Outpost/Cookie Kinkead; 123 Maura McEvoy; 124 Tim Street-Porter;125 Michael Mundy;126 Al Maha; 127 above The Interior Archive/Ken Haydn; 127 below Maura McEvoy; 128–129 Wharekauhau; 131 Preston-Schlebusch; 132 Ricardo Labougle; 133 Columbus Communications Island Outpost/Cookie Kinkead.

New Arrivals

134–135 Preston-Schlebusch; 137 Tim Street-Porter; 138 above Tim Street-Porter; 138 below Undine Prohl; 139 Undine Pröhl; 140–145 Lanny Provo; 146–149 Francesca Sorrenti; 150 Robert O'Dea; 151 My Hotel; 152 Conran & Partners; 153 My Hotel; 155–157 Hotel de Russie; 159 Blakes Hotel, Amsterdam; 160 above Taverne Agency/Mirjam Bleeker (Production Frank Viser); 160 below Blakes Hotel, Amsterdam; 161 Taverne Agency/Mirjam Bleeker (production Frank Viser); 162 Taverne Agency/Mirjam Bleeker (production Frank Viser); 163 Blakes Hotel; 164–165 David Collins/Andrew Lamb; 166–167 Claridges; 169–171 The Spa at Mandarin Oriental Hyde Park/George Apostolidis, Heaven Pictures, Melbourne, Australia; 172–175 Medusa Hotel; 176–181 Undine Pröhl/architects Ten Arquitectos; 183–187 Les Publications Condé Nast/© *Architectural Digest*, France/Noelle Hoeppe; 188–193 The Morrison Hotel; 194–199 Guy Hervais; 197 right GLA/Hotel Lancaster/Guy Hervais; 201–203 GLA/Hotel Royal Riviera/Henri del Olmo; 204–205 Christoph Kicherer; 206 left Christoph Kicherer; 206 above & below right Les Publications Condé Nast S.A./© *Architectural Digest*, France/Vincent Knapp; 207 Les Publications Condé Nast S.A./© *Architectural Digest*, France/Vincent Knapp; 209–211 Preston-Schlebusch.

Every effort has been made to trace the copyright holders, architects and designers and we apologise in advance for any unintentional omission and would be pleased to insert the appropriate acknowledgement in any subsequent edition.